DISCOVERING MY ROYAL HERITAGE
HERITAGE
WHILE SURVIVING IN

BLACK SKIN

DISCOVERING MY ROYAL HERITAGE
HERITAGE
WHILE SURVIVING IN
BLACK SKIN

Webster E. Moore

CITI OF BOOKS

CITIOFBOOKS, INC.
3736 Eubank NE Suite A1
Albuquerque, NM 87111-3579
www.citiofbooks.com

Hotline: 1 (877) 389-2759
Fax: 1 (505) 930-7244

Ordering Information:
Quantity sales. Special discounts are available on quantity purchases by corporations, associations, and others. For details, contact the publisher at the address above.

Printed in the United States of America.

ISBN-13:	Softcover	978-1-959682-59-2
	Hardcover	978-1-959682-61-5
	eBook	978-1-959682-60-8

Library of Congress Control Number: 2022923567

For more information, please visit: *www.discoveredheritage.com*

Contents

INTRODUCTION. i

CHAPTER I

EMMITT TILL *1*

CHAPTER II

Los Angeles. *4*

CHAPTER III

MARTIN LUTHER KING JR *8*

CHAPTER IV

NORMS *10*

CHAPTER V

INTEGRATION. *15*

CHAPTER VI

NAVY. *22*

CHAPTER VII

Aerospace Corporation *26*

CHAPTER VIII

WATTS REBELLION. *29*

CHAPTER IX

University California Los Angeles *38*

CHAPTER X

NIGERIA *55*

CHAPTER XI

Cal State University Northridge *66*

CHAPTER XII

RODNEY KING. *70*

Chapter XIII

EGYPT. *72*

• *The Sphinx*

• *Pharaonic History*

• *Egyptian Kingdoms*

• *Pyramid of Giza*

• *Temple of Hatshepsut*

• *Temple of Karnak*

• *Temple of Abu Simbel*

• *Kemetic Chronology*

• *Bibliography*

BIBLIOGRAPHY. *112*

DEDICATION

I dedicate this book to my mother, Maggie Olivia Moore, who immediately moved me and my brothers out of the Jim Crow South after the lynching of Emmitt Till, giving me the opportunity toward a higher education, otherwise, this book would not have been written; to my late Father who sacrificed his life to bring his family out of the south, and to my children with their opportunity to evolve from whatever lessons they may be able to gleam from this manuscript.

I must acknowledge Jolena Johnson who used her professional skills to actualize my procrastination into written words.

I especially dedicate this book to my wife, Dr. Sylvia Spencer, who has provided me with the love, spiritual environment, and mental support I needed to complete this manuscript.

Unveiling Ancestral Connections: African American Man's DNA Unearths His African Royal Heritage

The author's journey in Black Skin crystallized as he traveled through Egypt and was stunned at his face-to-face likeness to the sculpture of the Egyptian Pharaoh, Ramsey II. In addition, the author recently watched an interview of Dexter Caffey, an African American from Atlanta on the "African Diaspora News Channel," whose DNA analysis directly linked his ancestral heritage to the Egyptian Pharaoh Ramses III.

Such groundbreaking discoveries defy conventional historical narratives that insist that the Egyptian Pharaohs were not BLACK while looking directly into the stone face of Pharaohs with Black features that match the authors as well as the DNA analysis of Dexter Caffey, evidencing that the Pharaohs were indeed Africans in Black Skin. The truth, backed up by facts brings to light the remarkable contributions of African civilizations to world history and encourages a more inclusive and accurate narrative of ancient Egypt.

Link interview: https://www.facebook.com/ watch/?v=598054925723731

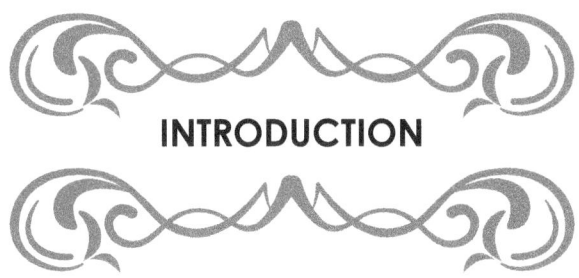

INTRODUCTION

"What became of the Black Pharaohs and Black people of Ancient Egypt"? the young student asked the Professor, "for ancient records show that the Egyptians & Pharaohs were Black,

The Professor sighed

"The younger civilizations severed their connection to the African high cultures that gave them birth; they expropriated all the sciences of Africa, suppressed and ridiculed her spiritual life, and in the process, buried the key to their own origins.

Gerald Massey
Ancient Egypt The Light of The World

"Now? Why now? I'm going into my senior year; can't we wait until I graduate?" Mom stopped ironing and looked directly at me:

"They just dragged a 14-year-old black boy out of his bed and beat that child so bad, his face was unrecognizable. Then they wrapped barbed wire around his neck, shot him in the head, hung him to a gin-fan, & then threw him into the Tallahatchie River,

simply because he whistled at a white woman; you're working at that restaurant around those white folks while they're in this killing mood. I'm getting you and your brothers out of the South now!"

I was entering my last year of high school when Mom and Dad abruptly sold our home, packed my two younger brothers and me into the back seat of a brand-new 1955 Chevy, and drove us out of the city of my birth, Mobile, Alabama.

Now, relocated into a Catholic high school in Los Angeles, California, I was dumbfounded when my classmates in white skins asked to see my tail, traumatized when the Catholic Nun told me in front of my classmates in white skin that my brain was only one-fifth the size of theirs. I joined the Navy, but the captain recoiled when he learned he had sailors aboard his ship in black skin. After the Navy, I was hired to install telephones for Pacific Telephone & Telegraph Company, but I was fired because customers in white skin refused to allow installers in black skin into their homes. I tried to buy a home for my family but people in white skins wouldn't allow people in black skin to buy in their community, etcetera. A craving evolved within me, to find th*e buried keys to unlock this unrelenting theme of white superiority.*

I flew from Los Angeles to New York to Amsterdam to Paris and finally to Egypt. Now here I am, standing on the grounds of Africa, the origin of people in black skins, and in Egypt, the origin of western civilization. I am surrounded by the ancient sands and stones of Egypt while looking up at the tallest manmade mountain of stone in the world, the Great Pyramid of Giza. The enthusiasm of our guide in describing what we're beholding, mirrored wonderment of what I am thinking about while standing on this historic site.

I thought of a line from Schwaller de Lubicz's great work, "The Temple of Man," wherein he stated, "Can any search for meaning be realized if it is not felt directly in our bodies?" That thought helped me understand this spinetingling feeling I'm experiencing right now, like a mystical linkage to those magnificent minds, and the amazing culture that built these immortal monuments. "Yes," my guide exclaimed, "you're looking up at six million blocks of granite stone, stacked so seamlessly, that mortar wasn't needed for a permanent bond.

"Each of these stones," as he walked over to one right next to me, "Averages six tons in weight alone." "Wow," I exclaimed, "these pyramids were calculated to have been built over ten thousand years ago." What an awesome view it must have been to observe these monuments then, especially the Great Pyramid with a keystone of solid gold at its peak, while its white limestone sides must have been dazzling as the sunlight played off its surface.

As my guide so elegantly stated, "There are simply no other manmade monuments more grandiose and temples more majestic, that have survived the test of time on this planet earth." When he said "manmade" I couldn't help but think of the people that did the making. The construction of these majestic temples and monuments, are certainly existing testimonials of the majestic civilization that created them. A civilization of people in Black skins that brought art, architecture, engineering, medicine, writing and government out of the native African lands of Nubia and Ethiopia, down into Egypt three to five thousand years before Greece and Rome existed.

A brief synopsis coming forward includes sculptured pictographs on the temple walls displaying the Egyptian holy family of Ausar, Auset, and Heru – Greeks renamed Osiris, Isis and Horus, Romans prototype for Joseph, Mary, and Jesus; the forty-two negative confessions—prototype for the Ten Commandments; the continual struggle between the Heru/Horus and Set, prototype for Cain & Abel; the mass exodus of the followers of Akhenaten after they lost the civil war between Upper and Lower Egypt, resulting in the prototype for the biblical Exodus; and the direct evidence that the characters in our biblical stories are in reality the stories of our African ancestors and their families, the stories of people in black skin. After all, the garden of Eden was in Africa and Adam and Eve were the original homo Sapiens which our anthropologists find in Africa, the birthplace of the human race. One of the greatest scholars to emerge in the African world in the twentieth century, Dr. Cheikh Anta Diop summed this up succinctly in "Civilization or Barbarism," where-in he wrote that: "Roman history is Greek, as well as Roman, and both Greek and Roman history are Egyptian because the entire Mediterranean was civilized by Egypt." Egypt in turn borrowed from other parts of Africa, especially Ethiopia.

I was literally stunned, devastated, and humbled by the monumental amount of knowledge I was exposed to; stunned at the architectural genius exhibited by the gigantic structures, down to the minute details embodied in the formation of humanity's first writing system - the hieroglyphs.

According to the Classical Authors of Antiquity, the country's name Egypt, sprouted from the Greek corruption of the name of some people in the ancient capital of Memphis - lower Egypt, which was Hwt ka pth which the Greeks pronounced as AEGUPTOS. That pronunciation was mistakenly applied to the whole country and by the time the Romans overruled the Greeks, the people of the whole country were called Egyptians. However, according to Professor Diop in "Ancient Egyptian Studies," most of the indigenous people called their country Kmt, when you add vowels, it is pronounced Kemet, meaning the Black Land. They referred to themselves as Kemitians, the black people. They called their writings, the "Medu Neteru." Meaning "Words of the Gods." The "Words of the Gods" seemed to literally permeate the very formation of ancient Egypt. According to Professor George James in Stolen Legacy(p1), "they regarded the human body as a prison house of the soul, which could be liberated from its bodily impediments through the disciplines of the Arts and Sciences, and advanced from the level of a mortal to that of a God." This was their very complex religious system called the Mysteries. So, their culture purpose, and goal, was about becoming, transforming from identifying only with the body, to identifying with the indwelling spiritual Self - Transcending from physical bodies to their original non-physical/ spiritual bodies.

So, it sounds like that non-physical/spiritual body was put into that physical/earthly body, eventually called a Homo-Sapiens, "to till the soil." Now I'm beginning to understand why the original Pharaohs in Black skin saw themselves as representatives of the Gods. Their lessons indicate they originally knew they were immortal spirits within mortal material bodies. That further explains why they saw death as a celebration, a resurrection into eternal life.

As I stood facing these incredible monuments and words of the Gods, I realized that every culture conveys their sense of identity, religion, and worldview to the next generation. Their temples were, and still are, a form of higher education. I felt I was in the largest legendary open-air art museum in the world, a significant center of learning. Indeed, Egypt was and is an awesome university. A university built before there was a written language, before there were books. Our most renown anthropologists, historians and Ehud Sperling, founder of the world's largest publishers of books, stated in the Temple of Man, (p.xiv), that "Egypt, not Greece, lies at the foundation of Western civilization." Egypt, inclusive of Ethiopia and Nubia, is authenticated as being the uncontested primary standard against which the early history of all civilizations was measured. After all, its southern borders are documented as the birthplace of humanity's ancient ancestors, the Homo Sapiens.

I was trying to decode the intended knowledge emanating from the sculptures, carvings, and pictographs, communicating through me, when I noticed a couple of Nubian men standing near a sculpture. They were dressed in white robes which seemed to be common wear amongst the Nubians. The sculpture caught my eye as I turned and fixated on how clear and defined the sculptured features were. I wondered; how could the clear details of its face survive over 3000 years without a scratch? I started walking toward the bust when both Nubians started pointing to me exclaiming, "Little Ramsey, Little Ramsey." One of them looked like he was around sixty and the other one was a lot younger, about twenty-five or thirty. I thought it might have been his son. Their skins were darker than mine, jet black, like ebony. This was true of all the Nubians I met throughout Egypt. They spoke a Nubian language from ancient Kush now called the upper part of Sudan. The Nubians are often referred to as the children of the ancient Kemitians.

I smiled and moved toward them, since they both were enthusiastically displaying such big smiles, while pointing at my face and then the face ofthe Sculpture. The older man then pointed at the Sculptured lips and then mine. Suddenly I got their message. Ramsey's African features, broad nose, notable facial projection in the jaw and large lips finally clued me in to the resemblance. Yes, I was suddenly in sync and a little stunned when I became aware of what they were excited about. I, for the first time, not only realized that this ancient Pharaoh's features were similar to mine, but even more momentous, I later thought that I could be carrying the genes of the most powerful and renown African Pharaoh that ruled ancient Egypt over 3,323 years ago. I wanted to talk more with the Nubians, but the language was too difficult, although they are known to speak in four different languages, but English generally, wasn't one of them. Historically, they were forced off their lands in the Nile valley because of the construction of the Dam which forced 50,000 Nubians into inner Egypt, the rest moved further south below the Sahara.

I reflected upon the litany of historical events that moved me from the Northeast coast of the continent of North America to the Northeast coast of the continent of Africa. Specifically, from California to Egypt. I'll start with the brutal lynching of Emmitt Till; the Catholic Nun's assault on my genetic intelligence; then witnessing the Watts Rebellion; and meeting with Malcolm X only to behold his and Martin Luther King Jr's assassination. In the same year, I was shaking the hands of Bobby Kennedy when he visited Watts in 1968 only to become aware of his assassination the following day, a couple of miles from my home. The following year the police brought a tank and a new Special Weapons And Tactics unit, S.W.A.T. into our community and had a shootout with the Black Panther's headquarters in my neighborhood, the following year I was beaten unconsciously by the police on UCLA's campus, I survived and some years later, I was able to meet with the anti-apartheid leader Nelson Mandela in 1990, after his release from 27 years of imprisonment in South Africa. The following year I was called to safeguard my youngest daughter, who was the lone juror that caused the conviction of two policemen for the brutal beating of Rodney King because he was in his black skin. Before I had a chance to process this unending litany of historical events, I received a letter from the Chancellor's office offering me a "Golden Handshake," i.e., an early retirement with benefits because my 55th birthday was approaching. I decided at that point to accept the "Golden Handshake" and fly into the land where people in black skin originated. I flew into Egypt.

Now that I am here, on this historic land, I am becoming aware that being in black skin is being in the skin color of my ancient Egyptian ancestors. The people whose genius became the foundation for western civilization. I felt and thereby knew I was truly with family, I felt "at home". I also came to the realization that my African American history isn't just about the 400 years of slavery, but it is about uncovering over 10,000 years of buried/concealed identity and historic accomplishments of my ancestors who laid the foundational stones inclusive of records, for other civilizations to follow. According to Cheikh Anta Diop, one of the greatest African scholars in the twentieth century:

Fourteen hundred years before Rome, Egypt created the first centralized empire in the world. (p85)

Therefore, a magnificent ascendancy of centuries and centuries of unacknowledged but well-documented Kings and Queens, i.e., Royal families in black skins for not one, but thousands of years. What is so extraordinarily beautiful, is that these ancestors left their imprint in granite stone that has not been possible to erase. Their statues, obelisks, temples, and hieroglyphs are written right in plain sight on the walls of ancient Egypt. These historical giants also built amazing libraries that housed the great knowledge from which the Greeks and later the Romans used to build their civilizations. I also learned that my ancient Egyptian ancestors didn't use vowels in their words. The term NG/Ng in ancient Egyptian meant lacking light, NothinG or No thing.

Their God's name was RA and all of life, all things emanate from God, from **N**o Thin**g**. When **Neg** is added to RA the word for Black is derived. **N**egra is Spanish for Black, Nero is Italian for Black, Negre is French for Black. The term Egyptian means the black people, they called their land "Kemet" or the Black Land.

"N-G-R" essentially meant "god" in ancient Egyptian language.

Once you input vowels you get: NeGRA. So, the original meaning of the "N" word had a connotation connected to the most powerful people on the planet being led by Kings, Queens, and Princesses in black skin. It is mindboggling to realize that every time a person used the "N" word to refer to a person in Black Skin, they were actually calling that person god! The Pharaohs were referred to as the "N-g-r-s" and the term "Pharaoh" meant the Great House called Per-o, and the Romans and Greeks pronounced it Pharaoh and they called the people in black skins "Nigers" meaning Blacks or people of African origins.

In summary, I discovered that people in black skins were not only enlightened cultured beings, but their leaders were revered as Gods in ancient Egypt originally called Kemit. They worshipped the ancient Egyptian Goddess Auset -Queen of the Gods, whom the Greeks pronounced as "Isis," but the indigenous Egyptian pronunciation was Auset, the Black Madonna.

I find that it's mind-blowing that for thousands of years people in white skins not only sought-after people in black skins in the Ethiopian, later Egyptian empire, but they saw those people in black skin as an advanced civilization. In 1955 B.C.E (**B**efore the **C**hristian Era), they went to the land of the black skin people, the *Ngras*, for literature, medicine, food, and prosperity. Even the biblical Babylonian Abraham willingly went into upper Ethiopia/Egypt offering his own wife to the Pharaoh in black skin as a gift.

But now, in **1955 C.E.** (**C**hristian or Common **E**ra), because of the color of my skin, my mother had to move me to safety like Isis had to move Osiris, and Mary had to move Jesus, to save my life because of the color of my skin. The threat of people in white skin lynching me and my brothers as they did to our neighbor in Mississippi, Emmitt Teal, terrified Mom. Emmitt was only 14, while Larry, my youngest brother, was 14, Spencer and I were 15 and 16. Mom was keenly aware that after the people in white skins lynched one young male in black skin, it became open season for lynching more "*Ngras*."

I heard all kinds of stories about what happened to Emmitt Till In 1955, however in this 20th century, the lynchings of human beings in black skin continues without any reduction in intensity: from Trayvon Martin, and George Floyd, to Tyre Nichols. According to Newsweek, Police officers killed 200 people in Black Skin in 2021 alone. Thanks to the media, the Emmitt Till-style murders are being exposed and documented.

In 1955 **C**hristian **E**ra, I was trained that if I looked a person in white skin in the eye, that act could get me lynched. It is so ironic that in 1955 **B**efore **C**hristian **E**ra, being in black skin was not only privileged, but there were royal families with Princesses, Kings, and Queens. In 1955 BCE, Ramsey II was 14 years old when his royal family granted him the status of Pharaoh; the boy, King Tutankhamen, was 8 years old when he became the king in black skin; the Pharaoh; Hatshepsut, the female in black skin that became a Pharaoh, a King and a Queen at the age of 12, she ruled the Egyptian Empire for over 20 years *(yes, she declared she was King and Queen)*. Akhenaton, the Pharaoh in black skin that is noted for fortifying Monotheism and seeding Judaism,

Christianity, and Islam, was around 15 years old when he became the primal leader of the Egyptian Empire. The list of Pharaohs in black skin over thousands of years is too extensive to cover in this Memoir. Consequently, the most exasperating question is…**What Happened?**

King Tutankhamen 1333　　*1Queen TyreKing Tut's-Grandmother*

King Tut's Father
- Pharaoh Akhenaten

Pharaoh Seti and his young son, the Crown Prince Ramses, later to become Ramses the great, confront their Heritage in a wall relief in a temple at Abydos. The carvings include the names of 76 Kings enclosed in cartouches running from the inception of Seti's reign in 1306BCE, all the way back to Menes, (First Dynasty) in 2920 BCE.

But, even worse, how did this highly advanced Black civilization completely flip on its head to where its people found themselves totally beholding to the people they brought civilization to. How did even the color of their skin become so substandard, just to mention the word black or the "N" word, was and is reprehensible!

In short, no books or other studies in my grade schools, high schools, college, nor universities ever offered any clues or answers to these questions. That was true in my schooling, the schooling of my children as well as the schooling of my grandchildren.

Now, living through the movement **"Black Lives Matter"** brings me to this living Memoir wherein I'm attempting to contemplate how the episodes in my lifetime, from the lynching of Emmitt Till in 1955 Christian Era., led me to Egypt to grasp the status of people in black skin Before the Christian Era, while continuing to breathe through today's brutal lynching of the George Floyds and murders of the Breonna Taylors in the twentieth century. Even as I'm editing this manuscript, February 2023 Christian Era, I'm looking at the funeral of Tyre Nichols on television. Tyre was another young man in black skin who was brutally beaten to death this time by five police officers in black skin. The video graphically displayed officers wildly punching Tyre, stomping on his body, kicking him in the face, lifting his body up in order to strike more blows to his face with their fists. Such a wild frenzied beating certainly brought to my mind the brutal stomping and beating to death of Emmitt Till which initiated my journey.

These Officers in black skins were obviously seduced and infected by the badge of power and authority. They were blinded by the fundamental social fact that they were assassinating a reflection of their own selves. All five of them were immediately fired and "charged with second-degree murder, two counts of official misconduct, two counts of aggravated kidnapping, one count of official oppression, and one count of aggravated assault." In a sense, that was the systemic destruction of six lives in black skin.

CHAPTER I

EMMITT

There have been too many different versions of exactly what happened to that 14-year-old from Chicago named Emmett Till, when he visited his cousins in Mississippi. I am now quoting directly from Simeon's Story, written by Emmett's cousin Simeon Wright. Simeon was in the same room when the two men in white skin kidnapped his cousin whom they called Bo Bo. I'm substituting (Emmitt's) real name rather than his nickname (Bo Bo) in the story. Simeon, who was present at the trial, wrote:

We were still excited about the day (picking cotton & swimming) and happy to be in town together... [We] stopped at the Bryant's store and Emmitt went in the store to buy a pop or something. Maurice (Simeon's older brother) immediately sent me into the store to be with (Emmitt)......... He just didn't know the Mississippi rules, and Maurice felt that someone should be with (Emmitt) at all times... While I was in the store, (Emmitt) did nothing inappropriate. He didn't grab Mrs. Bryant, nor did he put his arms around her-that was the story she later told to the court. A counter separated the customers from the store clerk; (Emmitt) would have had to jump over it to get to Mrs. Bryant. (Emmitt) didn't ask her for a date or call her "baby." There was no lecherous conversation between them. And after a few minutes he paid for his items, and we left the store together.

We had been outside the store only a few seconds when Mrs. Bryant came out behind us, heading straight to her car. As she walked,

(Emmitt) whistled at her. I think he wanted to get a laugh out of us or something. He was always joking around... It was a loud wolf whistle, a big-city "whee wheeeee!" and it caught us all by surprise. We all looked at each other, realizing that (Emmitt) had violated a longstanding unwritten law, a social taboo about conduct between blacks and whites in the South.

Suddenly we felt we were in danger, and we stared at each other, all with the same expression of fear and panic. Like a group of boys who had thrown a rock through somebody's window, we ran to the car.

It was two in the morning when Mr. Bryant and another white man (J.W. Milam) with a gun in his hand, forced Simeon's "Dad" to wake Emmitt (BoBo) up....Although Dad had two shotguns in his closet, he never tried to get them. If Dad had made a break for his guns, none of us would be alive today. Milam and Bryant were prepared to kill us all at the slightest of provocation. I am glad that Dad didn't do anything to put us all in danger....They took "Emmitt" out to a car or truck that was waiting in the darkness. One of the men asked someone inside the vehicle if this was the right boy, and Dad said he heard a woman's voice respond that it was.

Then they drove off...

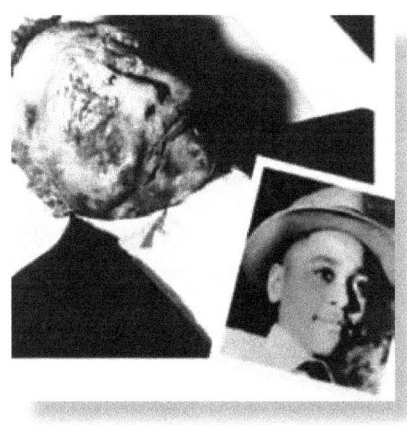

Three days later, they found what was left of Emmitt Till's body.

His face was unrecognizable.... the medical examiner reported there was extensive fracturing of the cranial skeletal remains. The medical examiner concluded that "Emmitt" had died from a gunshot wound to his head and that the manner of death was "homicide." Emmitt's was so savagely beaten and his head so swollen that his brain had to be removed before his body was shipped back to Chicago.

In 1955, to be on a jury, you had to be registered to vote. Black residents comprised 45% of the population of Tallahatchie County, but none were permitted to register. Thus, none could serve on a jury.

In my hometown of Mobile, Alabama, my parents often discussed the consequences for Black residents who registered to vote. If you registered to vote, your name and address was published in the local newspaper.

Your family was harassed, you lost your job, or you were killed. . Black people in Mississippi faced similar threats, so it was normal to have an all-white jury.

The National Association for the Advancement of Colored People (NAACP) sent Medgar Evers to meet Emmett's cousins and help locate witnesses. Evers was the NAACP's field secretary, as well as a distinguished Black WWII veteran. He helped Emmett's mother identify her son's body. He encouraged Simeon's father to testify, even though white residents had threatened that "he'd never live to see his next birthday." "It was the first time in the history of the state that a Black man had stood up in a courtroom and accused a white man of anything." Medgar Evers was later shot by a white Klansmen, in his own driveway, and killed.

The town sheriff conspired to protect the Emmitt Till's killers.

He hid the killers in his office, hindered witness testimonies, and advanced the lie that Emmett's body was "unrecognizable." It took the all-white jury just one hour to find the killers innocent.

Throughout the South, racist violence mushroomed, open season had been declared against people in black skin. A Black person could be charged for any offense, regardless of its veracity. This was the cause of a mass exodus of people in black skin to sell their homes and leave the South. My parents drove me and my brothers to Los Angeles. Four years after Emmett Till's trial, over 21% of people in Black Skin had left Tallahatchie County.

Los Angeles

People nationally and internationally were exposed to the details of Emmett Till's murder. In my new integrated neighborhood in Los Angeles, 3000 miles from Mississippi, I heard people of different ethnic groups publicly talking about him. In the southern states, people talked about it but never beyond a whisper. Here, in L.A., people were glued to their TVs, witnessing the brutality of Southern violence towards Black people. They discussed it on their porches, in their stores, on the streets, in their homes. This is new, I thought to myself, "this is different. Maybe we are not so invisible as I once thought?"

The killing of people in black skin had never created this much attention before. There were over 3,441 documented lynching of people in black skin between 1882 and 1955. That adds up to at least one hanging per week for 73 years, without any significant coverage. Now, the killing of people in black skin was on television in every home across the country.

The echo of Emmett Till's whistle not only changed the path of my life while closing the curtain on my father's, but that fatal whistle also manifested the "big-bang" that launched the Civil Rights Movement. It became a beacon for the national and international television stations that exposed not only this child-abduction and brutal murder, but the unbridled preeminence of southern white superiority that was further illustrated by the murder of National Association for the Advancement of Colored People's (NAACP) field representative, Medgar Evers.

My Dad's dream of a better life in Los Angeles was immediately crushed when the Sears & Roebuck store in Los Angeles refused to honor his transfer from the Sears store in Mobile, Alabama. The Administrative staff at Sears was shocked when they saw that dad was a man in black skin! With his seniority and experience they would have to give him a position above many of them in white skins. They didn't know how to handle it, so they kept giving him tests, examinations to pass. "The tests were silly," Dad told us. "I knew more about the equipment than they did. I had even designed some of them."

They kept telling him that his position would be ready in two weeks, then the following two weeks; then the following two weeks; after two years of this. Dad finally accepted the realization that Sears & Roebuck was not going to allow him to work there. Men in black skins with Dad's skills and seniority were not working for Sears & Roebuck in 1955, not in Los Angeles. Dad was very adept at handling the overt racism of segregation, but this covert racism of integration killed him. He actually retreated within himself, cut off meaningful communication with his close friends and eventually went into a coma and died!

I would have a remarkably similar experience five years later after my honorable discharge from the U.S. Navy as an Electrician's Mate.

I had a wife and a set of baby twin girls when I applied for a position with Pacific Telephone and Telegraph Company in downtown Los Angeles. They looked at my service record, recognized my experience as an Electrician's Mate and immediately hired me as a Phone Installer in Beverly Hills where they had an opening. However, when I arrived at the Beverly Hills office, the supervisor there was stunned to see that I was in black skin. I was told clearly that I could not go into the homes of White people in Beverly Hills, so they sent me to Culver City. When I reported to Culver City, I was told that the Jewish community wouldn't be comfortable with me coming into their homes in black skin, so they changed my title and position from "Installer" to "Frameman." A "Frameman" was a technician who troubleshoots telephone terminals and connects wires on a wire-distributing "frame" to telephone numbers inside a building. I did that full-time for a year at night while I attended National Technical School full-time during the day to be certified as an Electronics Technician.

Things were working out quite well for me with family, school, and this new job until I noticed that as soon as I drove into Culver City, there was always a motorcycle policeman following me through the city right to the doors of my job. When I went home, the same cop followed me out of the city, every day! At first, he gave me a ticket for going 35 miles per hour in a 30-miles zone. I made sure I broke no infractions. It was strange driving 30 mph on a busy street where others were driving 40 mph.

I also noticed that during my lunch hour in the telephone company's cafeteria, he was watching me from another table. I quickly found out that his wife worked in the same building as I did on a different floor as a telephone operator. I was informed that this cop didn't appreciate a Black man working in the same building as his wife.

I didn't want to become a statistic wherein he would have some excuse to shoot me on his bad day, so I took all his tickets into a court in Culver City. I explained my situation to the judge and expressed my fears that this policeman might escalate these encounters and I wanted my concerns to be on the record. Luckily, the judge informed me that the officer had a reputation of harassing Black people, and he dismissed all the tickets. About a week later, I learned that the officer was transferred, and I never saw him again.

I met another Black man on the frame in Culver City. He came to Los Angeles from Detroit with a master's degree in economics. He found out that no bank, would hire him when he showed up for interviews in black skin. He and I became best friends, I even went with him on a few of his attempts to get an interview. When they saw his resume, they couldn't wait to hire him, however when he showed up, when they saw his skin color, they told him that there were no longer any positions open. He went from one bank to another and was told the same story, that's how he ended up here with me at Pacific Telephone & Telegraph as a "Frameman."

It is very interesting that years later, after the Los Angeles Rebellion, he was teaching classes in Watts, California. He's the person that called and asked me to come to Watts to show the young adults in black skin how the skills they learned in their classes could provide full time positions in the Aerospace industries as it did for me. Mr. Bryant was also the person that over six or seven years later asked me to come to Cal State Northridge where he was a professor teaching Economics in the Black Studies Center. I informed him about my meeting with Stokely and he used my information to get the black Study's Department to change its name to Pan African Study's Department.

MARTIN

1955 was the year of Emmett Till's trial and the year I was carried out of the South. It was also the year that Martin Luther King Jr. received his Doctorate in Systematic Theology, and then was chosen by the National Association for the Advancement of Colored People to lead the historic Montgomery Bus Boycott. That boycott was in response to the arrest of an NAACP secretary-the woman in black skin who simply refused to give up her bus seat to a man simply because he was in white skin. Her name was **Rosa Parks**.

Martin Luther King Jr. continued to lead the protest-ants into ending discrimination in public places (1964) and granting the right to vote to all Americans regardless of the color of the skin one might be wearing (1965). In 1968, his moral and principled standards matured into the call upon the United States Armed Forces to terminate the killing of Vietnamese people by ending the war in Vietnam! Like Medgar Evans, he too was assassinated (1968).

An interesting side note is that over 400 years earlier a German Biblical Scholar named Martin Luther also received his Doctorate in Theology and likewise led a historic group of Protestors. This was later called "The Reformation" and the birth of the "Protest-ant Movement."

He challenged the authority of the Pope of the Roman Catholic Church; translated the Bible from Latin into the language of the people, and "Resulted in his excommunication and condemnation as an outlaw by the emperor." His protesters in 1512 coined the term "Protestants." His followers are the Luther-ans.

It was interesting to learn that Martin Luther King's father had traveled to Berlin in 1934, to the same land where the German Martin Luther defied the Catholic Church. According to the story, Martin Luther King Junior's Father, became so inspired by the German reformer that he decided to change his son's name from Michael to Martin.

CHAPTER IV

NORMS

A cultural norm I inherited in the South was not whistling at a woman with white skin. That was a cultural norm that was fatal for males in black-skin - no matter their age. I couldn't even imagine whistling at a white woman any more than I would whistle at a female bear. This wasn't something that I had ever witnessed.

Living in a separate black community, prevented me from having relationships with people in white skin. When a child is brought into a family, he is immediately schooled or trained into the cultural beliefs of that family and then that ethnic group, and then that community and eventually the nation. However, my first-hand experience with integration in Los Angeles made me aware of the Southern cultural norms I'd inherited and prompted me to question them. Thinking back, my first lesson might have begun with a knock at the front door when I was around 8 years old. At the door was a young man in white skin, selling life insurance. This was my first memorable experience of my Father's face-to-face interaction with a male in white skin at our home. I will never forget the way my father reacted. Dad, who I knew to be firm and powerful, actually dropped his head, looked down at the floor and said "Yes, sir" and "No, sir." I was dumbfounded. I felt a creepy atmosphere of fear surrounding my father and creeping into me. I didn't understand it, but I knew I wasn't supposed to let him, or anyone know what I witnessed.

I've never talked about it, but I knew it was part of this "peculiar institution" we call the cultural norm. The message implanted into my brain was a neuron that said, "It's dangerous to make eye-contact with anyone in white-skin."

My Dad was one of the most respected men in the Black community.

He was well-read, educated, a great hunter, a family physician, a technician, a builder, a former boxer, and had even been a driver for a famous gangster named Al Capone. If facing a little man in white skin brought fear to him, then I accepted that there had to be some frightening consequences to do otherwise, consequences that must have been worse than the axiom "Don't look at the sun or you will go blind."

Whistling at a female in white skin or simply making direct eye contact was like trying to charm a python snake by looking into its eyes.

Why would any sane person do that? In my seventeen years I never heard anyone in black skin ever voluntarily doing that. This was a way of life, a way that became the norm within most American homes in black and white skin in southern states.

These cultural norms were so embedded into my southern upbringing that I never even thought people in white skins were of the same human stock. It never occurred to me to make eye contact with a crocodile, a snake, a bird, a bear, and especially not with a person in white skin. We lived in separate communities, governed by the southern "Black Codes," laws that replaced the social controls of slavery. The "Codes" assured the southern states of the continuance of the cheap and in most cases, free labor. Free or Cheap Labor is the backbone of "White Supremacy." I came across a quote from David Blight in his course on "The Civil War and Reconstruction" where he succinctly stated:

...by 1860, there were more millionaires (slaveholders all) living in the lower Mississippi Valley than anywhere else in the United States. In the same year, the nearly 4 million American slaves were worth some $3.5

billion, making them the largest single financial asset in the entire U.S. economy, worth more than all manufacturing and railroads combined. So, of course, the war was rooted in these two expanding and competing economies."

These two competing economies of subordinating people in black skin in order to make millionaires while mushrooming the financial assets of the entire U.S. economy illuminates why the entire institutions of the United States conspired in the subordination of people in black, brown, or yellow skin.

The Emancipation Proclamation was really a remarkable opportunity for the southern states to welcome in the newly achieved rights of its citizens in black skins. But to do that, they would have had to reject the competing economies. The thought of sharing their wealth caused the southerners who owned and controlled the means of production to passionately war against any kind of cooperative living. They would have to immediately accept people of African origin as equal human beings instead of "Chattel" that existed for the purpose of enriching their lives.

The Black Church emerged like the Egyptian phoenix which rose from its earthly fragments. It served as the keystone that not only nurtured the fragmented lives of these human beings in black skin, but it united them into actualized communities. The Black Church became the voice through which African Americans could communicate with their neighbors in white skin. It became one of the first forms of land ownership and financial support for Americans of Black skin, promoting the development of their communities in America.

In the Encyclopedia of Alabama, I read that "Black People in Mobile lived in an isolated world, utterly separate from whites in most aspects of life and even death, with blacks and whites being buried in separate cemeteries."

I wasn't aware that I lived in an "isolated world" then. This was simply the only world I knew. The public media was carefully controlled, we had our own movie theatres, barber shops, schools, doctors, drugstore, newspaper, recreational facility, library, and churches. Whenever

I stepped outside of "the black district" I faced "Black Only" and "White Only" signs on the public water fountains and restrooms, even in the public parks. I certainly couldn't sit in restaurants with people in white skins, but I could work as a bus boy and serve them, or as a dishwasher. My uncle Web even cooked their food as a private Chef.

I never knew any white people at all outside of the Catholic Nuns and Priests at my school, and at Constantine's Restaurant, where I worked as a busboy in downtown Mobile. Of course, I was never allowed to walk through the front door of that restaurant, nor sit with the white workers, not even when the restaurant was empty. When I walked home,sometimes I took a shortcut through the white neighborhood. It was always like going through the jungle without a weapon. The kids in white skin yelled "Nigger," and sometimes they threw rocks at me. I walked faster, kept my eyes on the pavement and held my breath until I made it through. It's kind of eerie, you wouldn't dare run because there would be the assumption that you did something wrong that would invite them to chase you. I didn't want to entice them any more than I would entice abarking dog, especially when they're off their leash.

Walking home one late night, after working overtime at the restaurant, I reached the main drag, Davis Avenue, and noticed two policemen in white skin pulling out their guns and shooting a poor old black guy in the back. No one was around but me; they started laughing like they were having fun and found something to shoot. They put their guns back in their holsters and simply walked away, leaving the guy lying in the allcy.

I never said anything to my parents, and I never heard anything about the incident. But again, one thing was clear, the lives of people in black skin were simply not significant to these white officers. Of course, there was no such thing as a black police officer in Mobile during my upbringing, and according to the black codes it was understood that a citizen in black skin couldn't take a person in white skin to court.

My Mother was a Maid for the Wilkersons, a rich white family in the suburbs. She would take me with her whenever she had to stay the whole weekend in the maid's quarters. They lived on Wilkerson Ave., their kids went to Wilkerson Elementary School and Mr. Wilkerson played golf on the Wilkerson Golf Course. I helped clean the horse stables at the "Wilkerson's Stables."

One weekend I was admiring a little car modeled after a Packard, the car company that Mr. Wilkerson owned in Mobile. His kids were having a birthday party on the grounds. They spotted me down in the driveway and they started throwing coins down at my feet yelling for me to dance for them. *"Dance, nigger, dance,"* they all shouted. I quickly made it back to the servants' area before one of them tried to make me pick up any of those coins! I never told my mother about that experience, but she found out about it from her brother, Webster, who was the Wilkerson's Chef.

She never took us back there again.

CHAPTER V

INTEGRATION

My first year in Los Angeles was also my last year in high school and my first experience with integration. Our family's movement into L.A. was like watching a stage show, illustrating our integration into the diversity of Los Angeles. The background of this scene would be the movement of Black people escaping out of the southern states while integrating into Northern and Western cities throughout the United States. The surge was so overwhelming that blues singer Nat King Cole immortalized the song Route 66, for those black travelers leaving Chicago going to Los Angeles.

My parents enrolled me into St. Agnes, a large white Catholic School in central   Los Angeles. I was not only embarking upon my last year of high school, but this was to be my first year of integration. However, I felt I was merging into a familiar and nurturing environment since I had been baptized and confirmed in the Catholic Church and 11 years in a Catholic school with a B-plus average. I remember that the southern nuns had even suggested to Mom that I might become a priest. However, I had never seen a black Priest, a black Madonna, a black Angel or a black Jesus, so that suggestion never emerged in the images of my mind. It was to be another thirty-eight years before I even discovered that Catholicism, the first Christian Church that had a profound influence in the development of European Culture, had actually originated in Central Africa, culminated in Northern Africa-Egypt (ca. 3000 B.C.E.), and transcribed by some "chosen people" into the language of the Roman colonizers (325 AD). I was just as shocked to learn that I was using the name of the Holiest of Holy African Gods "AMEN" in my prayers without any cognition that AMEN" was the "Egyptian God named by my ancestors over **5,000** years ago **B**efore **C**hristian **E**ra.

I was the only student in black skin in most of my classes. It was quite a contrast coming from a 17-year southern history of being raised only with people in black skins. In Mobile, Alabama, the doctors, the pharmacists, the barbers and the beauticians were all people in black skin. Everyone that I knew or met was in black skin, except for the Catholic Nuns at my school, the only school in our community that had teachers in white skin.

Now looking back, it is obvious that this was true for the kids in white skin too. They watched me as if I were the first Black kid they'd ever met. Whenever I went to the restroom, the boys in white skin looked hard at me whenever I dropped my pants. I wondered why they watched me so closely in the restroom. One day one of them came over and asked if he could see my tail. I really didn't know how to respond, they really thought I had a tail. I wasn't angry, it just reinforced how strange they thought I was. And it reinforced, too, how strange I thought they were.

Since I was used to being an active participant in the learning process in Mobile, I sat at a desk in front of the class, you might even say I was the "teacher's pet" in my former schooling in Mobile. I was an altar-boy—I was up early in the mornings serving mass during the week. I said the whole Mass in Latin without knowing the English translations. I came on weekends to run errands for the nuns in the convent.

I was always considered the ugly duckling at school. The kids at school considered my skin too dark, and they reminded me every day that my lips were larger than theirs. They called me "Big Lips." I hated my features since they were so unattractive to my classmates. But they did appreciate my academic abilities. I got straight A's in all my math classes, and I just loved geometry.

The Southern Catholic School I attended in the city of Mobile was the only private school for kids in black skins. I now realize that most of the kids were from families that lived in a higher-class black community than mine. The kids in my community called "The Bottom," all attended public schools.

I noticed after looking at a picture of my kindergarten class, that most of my classmates throughout all my eleven years had lighter skin and/ or straighter hair than mine. When I was a teenager, I poured Clorox in my bathwater to see if it would lighten my skin. I put lye and water in my hair and conked it by buying a bottle of "King Conk." This was the most popular way guys in black skin straightened the curls out in their hair. The popular ones always had lighter skin and/or straighter hair.

In Mobile, the white Nuns seemed like missionaries doing charitable work in a foreign territory. This was clearly not the case with white nuns in their own community in Los Angeles. They didn't want any black kids in their classes. My Mother fought hard to get us enrolled at St. Agnes.

The racism I experienced in L.A. was more covert than the racism in the South, but it was similarly brutal and degrading.

My 12th-grade homeroom teacher, a Roman Catholic Nun, was lecturing on the structure of the family and the role of the Mother. She discussed how the female's brain is structured to focus upon minute details compared to a man's brain, which overlooks details and focuses upon broader issues. "This is necessary," she stated, "because the man is responsible for going out into the world to struggle with worldly matters, not tend with the details of homemaking."

I raised my hand. "I read that the differences depended upon whether the woman worked outside the home or not," I said. "If the guys stayed home and the women went out to work, then women would discuss worldly things and men would discuss the details of home. So, it seems that the difference wouldn't be the structure of the brain, but whether you worked at home or out in the world."

The face of this Roman-Catholic-Nun began transforming from white to pink to a glowing red. Looking directly at me, speaking in a determined, loud, but measured voice, she said, "Someone told you that and now you're trying to claim you read it. The size of the brain of Negro people is only a fifth of Caucasians, therefore you couldn't possibly have read and understood what you're saying." She then stood straight up and without taking her eyes off of me, folded her arms across her chest andslowly backed up. She said, "You've learned how to copy others and that's cheating. We will not allow cheating here."

I was petrified the entire time she was yelling at me. My brain was flashing images and sounds like a strobe-light at a disco, bursting out the names white kids used to yell at me whenever I walked through their neighborhood in Mobile, as well as the name calling we did amongst each other, in a degrading game called "the dozens." But they didn't sting like they did at this humiliating moment:

NIGGER! STUPID! IGNORANT! GO BACK TO AFRICA! BLACK-SAMBO! BIG-LIPS! YOUR MOTHER'S A WHORE! KINKY-HEAD-SON-OF-A-BITCH!

I flashed back on the scene at the filling station just as we pulled into Texas on our trip west. My Mother asked to use the restroom. The young white station attendant in a unconcerned tone said, "Go out in the field, niggers can't use our restroom." That feeling of being "The Invisible Man" is what I felt then, and it is what I'm feeling now.

Ironically, this experience also helped me understand the disquieting distance between black fathers and their sons in the face of society's negation of the black male. Finally, I realized that Dad was as helpless against that young kid at the filling station as I was against this messenger from the Roman Catholic Church.

This was my first negative encounter with Christianity. The second happened four years later when I was home on leave from the Navy and took my first kids, a set of twin girls, to be baptized at St. Cecilia's Catholic Church three blocks from my apartment. The priest refused to baptize my kids because I didn't have the correct "donation" he required for two baptisms. I could not believe that a man of God would send the souls of two children to limbo based upon a few dollars. That was the end of my faith in giving other people, Catholic or not, the awesome power over the destiny of the soul of my children and in the case of the high school nuns, the assumed right to determine the limitations of my intelligence.

My experience with the nuns caused me to move out of that front seat with the realization that my skin color completely blocked my identity. I retreated to the back of the class and never raised my hand again in that school. It was a change that stayed with me even till today. The stuff I keep buried inside, questions I want answers to but am afraid to ask. Even in social science classes and religious studies classes in the South, the nuns never answered. They simply told me that it was not necessary to understand anything, just have faith, believe, and remember whatever they taught. The priests told me to pray, and the Lord will guide me. That never worked for me from kindergarten through 12th grade. I even felt the same when I went into the armed services. I learned that if you're black, you're not supposed to know or question.

I left the Catholic Church and vowed that I would never allow them to distort the minds of my children. I didn't want them enduring the pain I suffered in jerking my mind out of the intrinsic and extrinsic conditioning I had believed in for 19 years. I didn't want them subjected to a group of unconscious teachers, so ensnarled into their own tribalism that they had completely discounted their own spiritualism.

It took a while, but I remember well the day I was able to pass a Catholic Church without making that habitual sign of the cross. That was the day I was released from a haunting fear of being barbecued in the fires of hell.

That was the first time I felt a sense of wholeness, not separated from Self, but completely responsible for Myself. It was a new, different feeling experiencing the guidance of my true spiritual self out of reason, not fear. This was a new awareness. It meant that I had to be responsible for what I did, for what my body was doing, even being aware of what my mind was doing. What clearly emerged in my reality was that I am not simply this body. There is a part of me that's capable of making choices without emotions, a part of me that's ready to take on the responsibility for my life rather than blindly following some old, learned patterns and rituals like a child.

I was walking past St. Agnes' Church one night and decided I wouldn't make the sign of the cross in passing. I heard my inner voice saying, "I will be responsible for you," and I believed it. I believed in my inner voice. I felt the weight of the chains fall from my mind; I literally heard the sound of chains hitting the sidewalk behind me. Having the sensation of lightness, I turned around looking down at the sidewalk, a new plane of awareness emerged within me.

I graduated from high school in 1957. At the beginning of that year, September 4, 1957, a young girl by the name of Elizabeth Eckford was denied entrance to Little Rock, Arkansas Central High School. The anger expressed by the white southern community was televised throughout the world causing the national attention of a person in black skin the same as the media did with Emmett Till.

After high school I enrolled in classes at Los Angeles City College. It's a strange feeling to graduate from a high school and not know what to do or where to go. It seemed that all the kids in white skin were going to college, but I had really no idea of what college was. In my hometown of Mobile there were no colleges open to people in black skin and I had never heard of anyone going to nor discussing college.

Los Angeles Community College was right on the streetcar line, two blocks from my house, so I enrolled. I majored in engineering because those are the skills my dad had. I joined the Students Engineering Club and tried to socialize and meet other students in my classes and in the Engineering Club, but the friendship never went beyond the campus. I was never invited to any socials, nor did I find a study partner. It was truly clear that wearing a black skin wasn't popular in 1956.

While riding the bus to college one morning, I noticed an ad forty-five degrees up, in the curvature wall of the bus. The words in Red, White, and Blue: "Join the Navy and see the World," were calling to me. I signed up.

CHAPTER VI

NAVY

This was the second big movement in my life. The first was **crossing** the United States from the Gulf of Mexico to the Pacific Ocean. This time I would cross the Pacific Ocean from the North American Continent to the Continent of Asia, including Hawaii, the Philippines, and Australia, covering over 6000 miles one-way.

I boarded the *U.S.S. Hancock,* an aircraft carrier with a crew of 3000 men. I signed up as an Electrician's Mate only to discover that sailors with black skins weren't allowed into technical divisions. I was immediately made a Boatswain's Mate. I was joining the sailors who make the nets, paint, clean, and dock the ship. I was disappointed but not surprised. I wasn't even allowed to take the necessary exam to increase my rank. However, once I managed to slip into the exam room and complete a test, without telling my Petty Officer. It didn't do any good, he found out, came into the testing area, and tore up the exam in front of the other sailors!

One day my Petty Officer called me into his cabin and said, "I see you went to college and now you're helping some of the guys with mathematical problems." "Yes, sir," I said. "Well, I don't want you helping another one of my men, and if I catch you teaching anyone in this division anything, I'll have you Court Marshaled."

Now I was surprised, this was ludicrous. But he kept his word. He found reasons to have me before the Court and incarcerated in the ship's brig at least twice a year.

While walking on Market Street in my Navy uniform, I was robbed by two men in black skin. They had a very sophisticated routine called a "pigeon drop." I had no idea what I walked into until I realized they had taken all the money I had on me. Of course, that was payday for Naval personnel, and I was foolishly exploring Market Street in my Navy uniform, like only a naïve sailor would do, with a pocket full of money.

I reported this right away to the police with a description of the robbers.

The San Francisco police later called me when I was back on ship. They asked me to come into the station to identify some suspects in a line-up.

I asked my Petty Officer for permission to leave the ship to go to the line-up. He not only gave me his permission to go, but he said, "Take the whole weekend off considering what you're going through."

When I got back to the ship Monday morning, I was put under arrest for being AWOL the whole weekend! At the Court Marshal my Petty Officer was adamant that he did not give me permission to leave the ship, so I was incarcerated in the Brig for seven days.

The brig wasn't a good place to be. The Navy uses Marines, to staff the brigs. I had experienced encounters with Marines off-ship whenever we went on-liberty in the different ports. In most of those encounters the Marines tried to demonstrate their Machismo, after a few beers, by provoking a fight. Once I was sitting with three other sailors drinking beers and a table full of Marines starting yelling obscenities at us. When they didn't get the kind of response, they needed they threw a chair at our table and then it was on. We beat all of them and left the bar before the military police arrived. They were too drunk to really defend themselves.

However, when I was sent to the brig, deep below decks, I saw that the marines' man and controls the brigs in the Navy. They ordered me to do 100 push-ups, which I was capable of at that time, then they had me shine the steal deck until I could see my face in it.

But the worst was standing at attention against the wall for hours and hours.

My ankles swelled up until they were as large as my knees. But I really felt sad watching other sailors who couldn't do the pushups. They laughed at them and called them "pussies." I saw them strip one black guy naked when he broke down and cried. They opened his cell and took turns abusing him.

From that experience I learned that the Marines respected nothing but physical power. So, I joined the ship's boxing group and rose to become the top lightweight boxer aboard. I knocked out one Marine after another in the ring. From then on, each time I was sent to the brig I would receive VIP treatment.

My popularity provided the opportunity for me to meet with a young Naval officer in white skin who had just graduated from the Naval Academy. He just happened to be an Officer in the Electricians Division. When I told him about my education and desire to be an Electrician's Mate, he saw to it that I was transferred right away.

We sailed to Hawaii, Guam, the Philippines, Japan, Hong Kong, and Australia. However, in 1959-'60, the government of Australia would not allow black sailors on their soil, so the Captain denied liberty to all the members of his crew with black skins. Consequently, I can't really say I was ever in Australia.

It was empowering, however, to experience people of color in other countries going out of their way to make sure that I received the best they could offer. I was always invited to elegant establishments, including their homes, places that even officers in white skins could not enter. I was also surprised at the level of knowledge people in other countries had about the treatment of people of color in America.

One black sailor was so captivated by the high level of treatment he received from the Asian people that he refused to leave. They had to incarcerate him aboard ship. When the ship was about 1000 miles from land, they released him. That black sailor jumped overboard and tried to swim back, rather than come back to America. The Captain sent a helicopter to lift him out of the water, but he refused to be rescued. We never saw him again.

On the other hand, it was disheartening to experience the arrogance of young white American servicemen toward people of color in every port we disembarked in. I was even more surprised when the guys I hung out with in white skins in the states, turned into completely different personas once we landed on foreign soils. One of my closest companions was a Catholic sailor who happened to be in a white skin, and at first his Catholic morals were seemingly parallel to mine. However, once we arrived on foreign lands these young Catholic boys turned into ravenousmale animals around women of color. Though they were married, theyslept with every prostitute they could as though they had never had sexbefore. When our ship left port, whether it was in the Philippines or Hong Kong, they lined up in sick bay because of the diseases they would encounter. The most popular disease was called "Non-Spec," which is a nonspecific autoimmune disease that sickbay couldn't even identify. It's strange that they had no fears of these diseases. Their superior attitude had no borders when it came to their sexual cravings.

I served two years on this far-eastern-tour when the ship's bow turned toward the United States, I was asked to continue for another two years with the Navy in Vietnam. I thought the offer was ludicrous. The racism in the Navy was so profound that I'll never forget the Captain blurting out over the ship's sound system that he can't wait "to get all these niggers off his ship." There were only a handful of sailors with black skins on that ship, but it was an unflinching announcement that caused my skin to crawl at the time hearing all 3000 members of the crew getting that unguarded denigration for no apparent reason. However, beyond that, I wasn't about to go to Vietnam to kill innocent Vietnamese people whom I didn't even know. They had never done anything to our country that I was aware of. I said no and returned to the states.

CHAPTER VII

Aerospace Corporation

I returned home to my wife and a set of twin girls. I knew I had to buy a home and raise my family so I couldn't return to college, so I went to work for Pacific Telephone & Telegraph during the day while going to National Technical School at night to be certified as a radio and Television Repairman. The industry was moving from vacuum tubes in radios and televisions to Solid State Electronics. I knew I would always find employment with that certificate in hand. I graduated at the top of my class and was hired by Aerospace Corporation in El Segundo California as an Electronics Technician.

This was my dream job. I had always dreamed I would be working in a laboratory wearing a white coat with top scientists. This is exactly what this position called for. I was hired to overlook and keep in repair an Electron and a Proton "Paramagnetic-Resonance-Spectrometer." This was pure research for the Air Force. They wanted to discover a material to use to coat the Space Vehicle, which they planned to use to send men into outer space. The material had to be able to keep the men cool when the vehicle got closer to the sun and warm when it passed to the cool side of the moon. The Air Force wanted to build a space station that could essentially monitor any country that threatened the United States, specifically, Russia.

My job was to handle all the electronics involved in this research and prepare the chemical samples provided by the Physicist whom I assisted.

On a side note, I was shining a beam of light through a crystal one evening and for a moment I was struck by the array of frequencies/colors emanating from the other side of the crystal: Red, Blue, Green, Yellow, and Purple. My immediate thought was these different colors could be people with different skin colors. The source of light emanating from the black box was equally distributed or individualized within each body on the other side of the crystal. The only difference between them were the wavelengths or frequencies which caused the different colors. But they all originated from the same black box. According to the geneticist Daniel Fairbanks, "Everyone's ancestry is ultimately African." So my observation of the different colors of light on the other side of the crystal all emanating from one black box or black body, brought to my mind how the different colors of people throughout the world happen to all emanate from one black body, from the continent of Africa.

During the five years of my employment at Aerospace Corporation, I was the only person in black skin that I had seen, not counting the janitors. I made very good friends with another technician whose degree was in physics. He grew crystals for the Proton Spectrometer. We became very good friends. We worked together, played together through the company's golf and chess club, visited each other's family, for years. Then one day we both walked with our wives, through a model home and our wives fell in love with the homes and the location. So, we both went in to pick the models we wanted to buy for our families. The gentleman in charge of selling the new homes looked at me and said, "I'm sorry but we can't sell any of these homes to colored people." My friend in white skin backed away from me and walked away.

When we met at Aerospace the next day, he told me that he was sorry, but he and his wife really wanted to buy one of those homes and he couldn't be seen with me. Otherwise, they might not sell his family a home.

I felt betrayed, hurt, confused about the conditional nature of friendship and more specifically, the paradox of integration. I flashed upon that Catholic Nun who insisted that even my brain was less functional than hers simply because of the color of my skin. I thought of when my Father was denied his transfer with Sears after they discovered a well-functioning brain but housed in an undesirable black body.

I joined the "Congress of Racial Equality." They taught me techniques of nonviolent behavior, how to not flinch when spat upon when sitting at a "White-Only" lunch-counter or standing in front of "White Only" new housing complex. We picketed all the new housing units built by this racist builder. After sells dropped significantly for this builder, he removed the color requirement. But it took a lot of dedicated members of CORE putting themselves on the picket lines and taking a lot of disgusting abuse. I remember observing an extremely angry white man screaming racial invectives into my face so close I could feel his spit hitting my face with every consonant. The anger and pain he was experiencing was so deep that I felt sorry for him at that moment because, like the Nun, he had no idea who I was nor the profundity of the historical moment. I was really having an out-of-body experience and it really felt like an extraordinary "high."

CHAPTER VIII

REBELLION

"The slave went free;
stood a brief moment in the sun;
then moved back again toward slavery."
(Dubois 1935)

The Congress of Racial Equality (C.O.R.E.) was inspired by Mahatma Gandhi's protest strategies of nonviolence and civil disobedience. The group worked alongside Martin Luther King Jr. and other civil rights groups taking a leading role in sit-ins, picket lines, the Montgomery Bus Boycott, Freedom rides, and the 1963 March on Washington. These continual movements out of slavery toward equality forced President John F. Kennedy to propose the "Civil Rights Act" in 1963. The southern congress refused its passage causing Martin Luther King Jr. to bring together more than 200,000 people at the Lincoln Memorial to demand equal justice in his famous "I Have A Dream" speech on August 28, 1963. Three months later, President Kennedy was assassinated – on November 22, 1963. Kennedy's Vice President, Lyndon B. Johnson, was sworn in as President of the United States and on July 2nd, 1964, he signed the Civil Rights Act into law on July 2nd, 1964.

However, the long-held tensions between the authorities in white skin and the impoverished Americans in black skin in the Watts neighborhood in Los Angeles, California heightened even more with the assassination of President Kennedy, and then on February 21st, 1965, the assassination of Malcolm X. It didn't take much to ignite the impoverished citizens. So when they watched a woman in black skin whom they thought was pregnant, fighting the police, other citizens jumped in to protect the woman causing more police to be called in, and before you know it that was the match that ignited the Watts Rebellion of 1965.

The Watts Rebellion in Los Angeles (1965) was documented as the most serious racial outbreak ever in the United States of America.

Eventually, the California National Guard was called to active duty to assist in controlling the rioting. On Friday night, a battalion of the 160th Infantry and the 1st Reconnaissance Squadron of the 18th Armored Cavalry were sent into the riot area (about 2,000 men). Two days later, the remainder of the 40th Armored Division was sent into the riot zone. A day after that, units from northern California arrived (a total of around 15,000 troops). These National Guardsmen enclosed a vast region around South-Central Los Angeles, declared martial law and mostly ended the rioting by Sunday.

I drove through the streets in Compton and Watts seeing the people happily burning and looting property like it was a great drunken party. The community for miles looked like a war zone but with no causalities, I felt I wasn't in the United States but in some strange dream.

The aftermath of the Rebellion prompted the President of the United States to invest 30 billion dollars into educational institutions to move the rebellious black citizens off the streets of the cities and into the fabric of society. In spite of forty (40) million dollars in damage, the rebellion sparked a sense of brotherhood, a sense of belonging. I was walking down Broadway, a street in south Los Angeles, when I passed a man in black skin. He said, "Hi, Brother," and kept walking. That seemingly simple salutation completely changed my humanity. For the first time in my life, I felt that I actually belonged. My people recognized me, and with pride and joy they embraced me. It sounds preposterous, but I really never had that unique feeling before. I went into a nightclub in my community on Jefferson Ave., and a singer by the name of James Brown was on stage singing: "I'm Black and I'm Proud." I could hardly believe it, that is exactly what I felt when a stranger looked at me and said, "Hi, Brother." The song became the number-one Rhythm & Blues hit almost overnight. It was as though a whole race of people came "out-of-the-closet."

However, it was quite uncanny that my facial features became desirous as a black male overnight. One day my features were ugly and the next day they were popular, like a movie star - big lips and all. Simply because my facial features were on TV.

The power of the social media verifies the impact of displaying the Pharaohs in Black Skin, their true colors, rather than the white, red, and yellow skin colors perennially displayed in movies & the history channel.

The "Watts Rebellion" spread from Watts 1965 to Chicago 1966, and Newark 1967. Then on April 4th, 1968, Martin Luther King Jr. was assassinated. American citizens in black skins revolted in more than 100 cities throughout America. President Johnson, who had already pushed through the Civil Rights Act of 1964 and the Voting Rights Act of 1965, formed the National Advisory Commission on Civil Disorders. One of the most famous warning from the Commission's study was that:

> Our nation is moving toward two societies, one black, one white— separate and unequal. What white Americans have never fully understood but what the Negro can never forget is that white society is deeply implicated in the ghetto. White institutions created it, white institutions maintain it, and white society condones it.

The Report called upon the government: to construct new housing, stop de-facto-segregation which creates destructive ghettos. It went further by recommending government programs to needed services, hiring more diverse and sensitive police forces and, most notably, to invest billions in housing programs aimed at breaking up residential segregation.

Educational Opportunity Programs were initiated on college and Universities campuses, Technical Schools called "Skill Centers" were established for citizens in black skins to teach employable skills.

I received a phone call from Vern Bryant, the friend I met on the "Frame" at Pacific Telephone and Telegraph Company. He taught at the Watts Skills Center. He touched on the critical needs of that community and asked if I would visit the school and speak to the students about education and job opportunities in the array of aerospace industries throughout Los Angeles. I accepted the speaking engagement not knowing the overpowering affect it would have on my life's trajectory. I was surprised to discover a sense of fear in their faces, a fear of the unknown. These students had never even ventured outside of their community, apart from going into the local Penal Institutions. A large portion of the population of the students at the Watts Skill Center were youth in black skins, that the public schools couldn't handle. There were also adults whose release from prison was contingent upon attendance.

My visit to Watts opened my eyes to the reality that most of the citizens in black skin in south Los Angeles had never travelled outside of their community. This was truly the meaning of the term "Ghetto"—an environment of isolation and desolation. I learned that the city buses only ran north and south, not east nor west. The bus lines into the black communities were designed to take the women from South Los Angeles to Beverly Hills to clean the houses and care for the children of people in white skin and return them back to their communities. There were virtually no job opportunities for the citizens in the Ghetto. Like the South, they were only there to serve the white communities.

If you didn't have a car you were isolated from one generation to the next. I'd never seen such poverty and lack of hope and direction. It was patently clear why the community exploded into an angry revolt, like the uprising in Egypt, in Tunisia, in Bahrain, in Syria, and in Jordan. Talking to the principal and the teachers, it was clear that education was the only foreseeable way out for citizens in black skin. The community was overrun with churches, liquor stores, drugs, and gangs.

The Principal, Ted Kimbrough, of Watts Skill Center asked if I would consider taking a leave of absence from Aerospace Corporation and work with the school, the teachers and students. Aerospace Corporation, my place of employment, understood and granted me a 6-month leave to teach in Watts.

One morning one of my students came to class with blood all over his clothes. He said the police didn't believe he was on his way to class that early and just decided to beat him for lying! I left immediately and went over to the 77th Precinct office, identified myself as a teacher at the school and reported the beating of my student. The cops around the desk simply laughed. I stated that I wouldn't leave until I put my complaint on paper.

I was handed a form, I filled it out, handed it back and the uniformed desk clerk simply balled it up and threw it in the trash can.

I left Aerospace and went to work in Watts full time, even though the teacher's salary was significantly less than what I was making at Aerospace. I felt that if I was going to "give back to the community," this was the time to give back. If I quit Aerospace Corporation the Apollo spacecraft would still enter outer space; if I stayed with Aerospace, I would lose my opportunity to give back to my community.

I taught electronic mathematics, electronic assembly, and drafting.

My students were challenging. They were cynical that education and skill-building could change the conditions of their lives. They came from rough backgrounds, and although they received a stipend for attending, they didn't take the initiative to study. To grapple with the racism, they were experiencing daily was enough of a challenge—to inspire them and support their studies was an even greater challenge.

I discovered that the teachers themselves were receiving no medical benefits, even though they were employed by the Los Angeles City Board of Education. They were all afraid they would lose their jobs if they asked for the benefits that the teachers in the white communities were receiving. Even the Principal wouldn't ask the Board of Education for anything. He regarded his position as an opportunity to transfer out of the community into the "regular" school system after a year or two of experience in Watts, i.e., he didn't want to jeopardize his promotional goals. I was to learn that that attitude was a fear, a virus that had permeated the faculty throughout the academic institutions from secondary to community colleges throughout the Cal State and the UC academic faculties. I joined the Los Angeles Teachers Association and immediately became a Union Representative for the teachers in South LosAngeles.

I was surprised when I went downtown and reported the lack of benefits for the teachers in South Los Angeles. The Director of the Board of Education said such a problem had never been brought to his attention. Within a month the teachers were given medical, vacation, retirements, and all the other benefits that teachers received in the "White" communities.

In many of the liberal studies classes the female teachers were experiencing a rough time controlling their classrooms. One of them came to my class and asked for help in controlling her students. I opened the door and found students playing dice on the floor. One had actually pissed on the wall while the teacher was trying to teach English. I had no such problems in my class because only the students who were serious about learning were allowed to sit in my room.

One class day a teacher busted into my class asking for help because a student had pulled out a switchblade knife and threatened to kill anyone who tried to take it! He hid in a bathroom outside of the principal's office. I noticed that no one dared go in and the student wouldn't come out. They were all congregating outside. I immediately went into the restroom and closed the door behind me. The student stuck the switchblade in my face and I could see in his eyes and his shaking hand that he was scared and had no idea how to get out of the mess he'd created.

I said, "You're not going to cut me because you would be arrested so, give me the knife and walk out of here and I won't call the police." I told him he could tell his friends I overpowered him and took the knife, so they won't think he simply gave me the knife. He agreed, we made a scuffling sound and walked out. That was the end of it.

MALCOLM X

I had been working with the pioneer of the Civil Rights Movement—
"The Congress of Racial Equality" (CORE) in Los Angeles, in support
of over 70 thousand students who sat-in, marched, and some who even
died while practicing nonviolent civil disobedience. It was Malcolm
X, however, who lifted me to a new horizon.

Malcolm X was set to give a talk at a church in my neighborhood.
I heard his "Message to the Grass-Roots" speech he gave in Detroit
where he contrasted the "House Negro" and the "Field Negro." He
explained how the field Negros prayed that the master would die when
he got sick and if his house caught fire, they prayed that it would burn
down.

However, "If someone came to the house Negro and said, 'Let's go,
let's separate,' naturally that Uncle Tom would say, 'Go where? What
could I do without boss? Where would I live? How would I dress?
Who would look out for me?' That's the house Negro, but if you went
to the field Negro and said, 'Let's go, let's separate,' he wouldn't even
ask you where or how. He'd say, 'Yes, let's go.'"

But tonight, he was going to discuss the "Ballot or the Bullet." I won't
be listening to the radio or watching him on TV, I'll be sitting right
in the front row. I arrived at the church early, it became totally packed
with people in black skins so fast that many had to stand. Malcolm
stood next to the church lectern in a black suit and tie, while I became
transfixed on every word he was about to utter. He began introducing
himself by assuring us that he wasn't being attacked because of his
religion nor his politics, but he was being attacked simply because
he was black. That understanding alone captured my spirit. Then he
began telling us that this year might be the year of the ballot or the
bullet. He said this was because "Negros have listened to the trickery,
and the lies, and the false promises of the white man now for too long.
And they're fed up. They've become disenchanted. They've become
disillusioned. They've become dissatisfied, and all of this has built up

frustrations in the black community that makes the black community throughout America today more explosive than all of the atomic bombs the Russians can ever invent." Malcolm really got the people to seriously look at the power and significance of their vote.

He convinced us that we needed to make a choice between the ballot or the bullet: between violence or nonviolence and that "Inaction was not acceptable."

The nonviolent movement practiced by C.O.R.E. laid one of the foundational stones for the Civil Rights Movement, but I began engaging with a new generation of activists in Los Angeles. Huey Newton's Black Panther Party, Malcolm X's Black Muslims, and Ron Karenga's US Organization all came together and formed the Black Congress Organization in South Los Angeles, chaired by Walt Bremont. This Community Organization corralled the youth gangs, dropouts, students, teachers, politicians and actually "managed" the political decisions coming out of South Los Angeles.

ASSASINATIONS

Martin Luther King Jr. was assassinated April 4th, 1968. That summer of the same year, I shook the tender hands of Bobby Kennedy as he walked on the streets of Watts assessing the damage from the Watts Revolt, as he campaigned for the Presidency. The next morning, he was shot at 12:15 A.M. at the Ambassador Hotel, about five miles from my home in Los Angeles. He died on the way to the hospital.

His brother, John F. Kennedy, the President of the United States, was shot to death in 1963. Malcolm X was shot to death in 1965, Martin Luther King Jr. was shot to death April of 1968 and Robert (Bobby) Kennedy was shot to death two months later, June 1968. These four assassinations of two leaders in black skins and two leaders in white skins, all within six years, shocked the nation. It uncovered a dark and deadly presence of a "subversive right-wing Power" usurping the leadership of the United States Governmental apparatus.

OPERATION BOOTSTRAP

In 1965, after the Watts Rebellion, a community-based organization called "Operation Bootstrap" was initiated in the Watts neighborhood of South-Central Los Angeles on November 24, 1965. This project held sensitivity sessions in which people from various communities, mainly people in white skins, were invited into the community to dialogue about solutions to help alleviate the problems in Watts. I volunteered to lead some of the sensitivity sessions when one of the participants invited me to lead a discussion in the all-white community of Sherman Oaks. I accepted the invite and while driving to the location down Ventura Blvd. on a Sunday afternoon, a motorcycle cop turned on his terrifying siren and blinking lights. I hadn't done anything to deserve being pulled over except driving through this white-skinned suburb in black skin. Coincidentally, I had just finished listening to Spencer, my brother, who called to share with me his pain and disgust at being stopped and harassed by the Los Angeles police simply because he was driving in black skin. The amount of money and dignity, we've forfeited through years of daily harassment begins to challenge one's self-identity, am I simply this black-skinned body to be toyed with anytime these guys in white skin wants to play their superiority game? This time my inner guidance system said "No, you don't have to play. Stand your ground!"

I pulled over into a parking lot rather than stopping on the busy street to prevent any distractions. The cop followed. I watched him get off his motorcycle through my rearview mirror, and without any thought, opened my car door while my hand reached down beside my seat and grabbed a tire iron. The decision had been made that I was not going to get this racist ticket, not this day. I stepped out of my car, faced the cop with the tire iron raised to my chest, ready to engage. The cop looked at me, looked at the raised tire iron being held firmly in my hand. He backed up slowly while maintaining eye contact, got on his motorcycle, and drove off. I stood there for a moment and let my inner rage subside, then climbed back into my car and drove to my session.

CHAPTER IX

UCLA

For two years I served in the South Los Angeles City School district as a teacher, union representative, and career guidance counselor, and I taught drafting and electronic assembly. My service was rewarding, but I felt compelled to re-enter higher education. The district needed a systemic change, and I didn't have the tools to initiate those changes. The schools were not offering its students in black skin a path out of the state-created ghetto. Nor a path out of the daily tyranny of police brutality.

The University of California at Los Angeles (UCLA) recognized the problem, after the release of the Kerner report denounced "white racism," and established an Educational Opportunity Program (EOP) in 1968. The EOP reached into the ghetto with its BSU recruitment arm and began enrolling previously marginalized citizens into the University.

I enrolled as a full-time student in January of 1969. I couldn't help noticing that the affluent UCLA neighborhood shielded the campus from the nearby ghetto. Beverly Hills was to the north, Westwood to the south, Hollywood to the east, and Brentwood to the west.

After living among only people in black skin, I immediately experienced a culture shock when I observed 99% of the university's population being people in white skins on and off campus. When I drove into Westwood, the police routinely pulled me over. Why was I there, they asked me. Once on campus, I was the only student in black skin in all my classes.

I became very friendly with a professor in black skin by the name of Dr. Tiyo Soga. He was from South Africa and was hired to teach in the High Potential Program on campus. He and I were walking together in Westwood when suddenly, a Westwood police car pulled up to us, got out of their car and asked for our I.D.'s. Dr. Soga tried to explain to the officers that he was teaching a class on campus and the officers became so enraged at Dr. Soga's English accent and his articulation that he quickly hit him in the mouth with his Billy-Club, knocking out at least one of his teeth, while yelling at him to shut up. He asked for my I.D. but then he purposely dropped my driver's license on the street and told me to pick it up. I said, "I gave you my license, what happened, I don't see it." I was not going to take my eyes off him. I thought he might hit me in the head when I stooped over, so he handcuffed me and arrested me. I was released the next morning.

I was so disoriented and captivated by my new classes, campus environment and simply going through the 1st stage of culture shock, that by the 3rd week of classes, I was suddenly and profoundly awakened with the news that two black students were shot to death right on campus, right in Campbell Hall where the EOP and BSU offices were located. The students were murdered within my first quarter of enrollment, in the same building and hallway I frequented.

It was in the winter quarter of January 17, 1969, when Bunchy Carter and John Huggins were fatally shot. The two students were leaders of the revolutionary Black Panther Party. UCLA locked down the site of the murder and boarded its doors. The dynamism of the BSU recruitment arm through the Educational Opportunity Program and the High Potential Program was disrupted. The BSU simply stopped meeting.

The former BSU officers were literally gun-shy, apprehensive after that terrifying shootout. Their parents informed them they were on campus to pursue an academic degree, not to be revolutionaries.

By that Spring Quarter of 1969, Ayuko Babu, presently the 'Executive Director of the Pan African Film & Arts Festival,' accompanied me when I tore off the boards blocking the entrance to the Cambell Hall building. I had decided to restart or reopen the business of the Black Student Union (BSU).

I simply took over as the Chair of BSU and coordinated a central committee composed of two community liaisons, Little Joe and Daktari and two UCLA students. Ayuko Babu, a law student, and another student named William. I facilitated the hiring of two UCLA Directors—Dr. Robert Singleton, a former Mississippi Freedom Rider, who was hired as the Director of UCLA's African-American Study Center, Dr. Al Solomon, a former teacher at the Watts Skill Center, who was hired as the Director of UCLA's Personnel Office, and Angela Davis, a radical feminist, member of the Communist Party USA via the all-black Che-Lumumba Club as well as an affiliate of the Black Panther Party.

Out of the ashes of the Los Angeles Riots and the assassination of Malcolm X in 1965, Huey Newton, Cofounder of the Black Panther Party (BPP) in Oakland and Bunchy Carter, founder and leader of the Party in South Los Angeles launched the BPP for Self-Defense in 1966.

I identified with Huey Newton's Black Panther Party. I admired their responses to the ceaseless police brutality and overt racism on the streets of Los Angeles. Ayuko Babu and I met with Huey in his home in Oakland, California. I was captivated by his recounting of his meeting with Mao Tse-Tung, the chair of the Chinese Revolutionary Party. This is why he introduced Mao's "Little Red Book" to the Black Panther Party. I often used the "Little Red Book" as a guide and quick reference in our BSU study groups along with President Kwame Nkrumah's Little Black Book. Nkrumah was the first prime minister and President of Ghana. Huey shared with us some of Mao's teachings.

Huey was an avid reader and philosopher. He is most remembered, however, for his supervision of the black neighborhoods. He patrolled the streets, armed with a sawed-off shotgun and a lawbook. He met citizens in black skins and reminded them of their Second Amendment right to bear a weapon. This presented an in-your-face challenge to the unrelenting tactics of the police department on unarmed defenseless citizens. The FBI smeared the Black Panthers as "the greatest threat to the internal security of the country."

I dressed in my black leather jacket and combed my natural just like Huey, Bobby Seale, Eldridge Cleaver and Bunchy. One morning I wore my Panther outfit, and a police car literally drove over the curb and onto the sidewalk on Western Avenue, three blocks from my house, and forced me against the wall with their car bumper. They got out with a gun in their hands screaming at me, "Who do you think you are?" I was simply dumbfounded. Wearing my Panther outfit in America, it turned out, waslike wearing red in front of a bull. It was very clear that anyone replicatingthe party's image was their enemy.

Bunchy Carter, leader of the Los Angeles Chapter of the Black Panther Party and John Huggins established the Party as a force in Los Angeles.

They provided a model for Self-Reliance and a sense of protection and dignity for men in black skins, and their breakfast programs provided healthy nutrition for the families.

I had reservations about getting too close to Ron Karenga because his ego was simply off the chart. He loved demonstrating his intellectual acrobats at every opportunity available. The only time I had the privilege of experiencing his unobtrusiveness was when Angela Davis and I attended a Black Alliance meeting in the community. I was amazed at his ability to be silent and attentive when he was in the presence of Angela.

However, I was really turned off one evening while observing one of his admirers kissing his ring hand as though he was the pope. On the other hand, I admired his genius, and I was then and now in total agreement with his campaign stressing the recognition and elevation of black culture and identity. His inauguration of Kwanzaa, now the African American holiday celebrated by millions throughout the world, is the keystone toward that effort. Nia, Karenga's 5th principle of Kwanzaa, stresses "the building and developing of our community to restore our people to their traditional greatness." Kwanzaa brings a cultural message which speaks to the best of what it means to be African and human in the fullest sense.

Karenga's cultural nationalists focused on language and traditional African dress, as well as the national holiday of Kwanzaa, it certainly established pride in our cultural programs throughout the United States as well as internationally.

 In the 1960s I personally met many of our trailblazers, including Angela Davis, Ayuko Babu, Bobby Kennedy, Louis Farrakhan, Malcolm X, Martin Luther King Jr., Huey Newton, Ron Karenga, Robert Singleton Stokely Carmichael, Jessie Jackson, Nelson Mandela, and Walter Bremond. These individuals struck me as truly self-actualized individuals.

They demonstrated leadership, courage, and a refusal to compromise. But their craving for knowledge, was especially profound. They spent years studying and completing their degrees before they assumed their leadership roles.

This wasn't easy in the 1960s as it is today in the 2020s. I'll just use two examples, Malcolm X and Huey Newton. Malcolm was illiterate, he couldn't read nor write before he became a Muslim. He expressed the profound thought that he had never truly been free until he fully understood how to read and understand literature. He literally taught himself how to read by remembering the meaning of every word in the dictionary.

Huey was illiterate when he graduated from high school. In his autobiography he stated that: "Not one instructor ever awoke in me a desire to learn more or to question or to explore the worlds of literature, science, and history. All they did was try to rob me of the sense of my own uniqueness and worth, and in the process nearly killed my urge to inquire." But, like Malcolm, that "True Self" within meticulously taught him to teach himself to read. He earned his AA degree, BA degree, Master's and Ph.D. while he simultaneously cofounded the Black Panther Party. Each of these trailblazers first became conscious of their own Self-Consciousness before mastering the language needed to guide their actions. The two Black Panther leaders fatally shot on campus, were following in the footsteps of Malcolm X and Huey Newton in their pursuit of higher education when they became students at UCLA. I experienced the same phenomenon when I left my career at Aerospace Corporation, as well as a teaching position in south Los Angeles to attain a higher education to better understand, like the renown Marvin Gay's hit song, "What's Going On."

In my position as the chair of the BSU student club on campus, I was able to check out an Official University Car and drive three of my newly installed central committee members to a Black Student Union Conference in San Jose, California. After driving approximately 150 miles on Highway 101, my rearview mirror and essentially the whole university car was flooded with intensely bright flashing-colored lights, followed by the incredible sound of sirens. I was extra concerned because there were more than one set of flashing lights. I alerted the guys in the back seat and immediately pulled the University Car over to the side of the highway. The police bullhorn ordered us to get out of the car with our hands up.

This was unusual, normally they would walk up to the car, tell me why I was stopped, and then request my driver's license and insurance. But that didn't happen. "Get out of the car with your hands up!"

I told Daktari, Little Joe and William to keep quiet and just let me do the talking. We got out of the car and noticed a line of police cars.

We were told to get out of the car one by one with our hands up over our heads. The cops were out of their cars, some laying on the ground on the other side of the street, pointing rifles directly at us. I noticed one cop looking through a scope on his rifle aimed directly at me. The police asked me what we were doing in a state-owned car. I told him I was Chairman of a student organization on the UCLA campus and I checked out the vehicle to attend a meeting at another state campus. He asked for my identification, I lowered my hands and gave him my driver's license. He called it in. We had to continue waiting with our hands up over our heads not moving. Finally, one of the cops received verification of what I said. Looking totally defeated he ordered his men to put away their weapons and said they thought it was a stolen car.

They had never experienced a car full of black faces driving in a car with an official-state-vehicle. I was so relieved that none of the guys mouthed off at the cops during this ordeal! Whenever you're dealing with a group of cops, it only takes one to "inadvertently" pull the trigger.

The 60's marked the assassinations of Malcolm X, Martin Luther King Jr., President Kennedy and his brother Bobby Kennedy. The citizens in black skins responded to these assassinations with a wave of race rebellions. Correspondingly the rise of the anti-war movement dramatically shifted the tone of the Civil Rights Movement. Stokely Carmichael seized upon the rhythm of this movement by coining the slogan "Black Power."

 Stokely first gained prominence in the early 60s when two Alabama policemen ordered him to stop handing out voter registration materials. Stokely stood his ground—he told the cops to either arrest him or to back off! The cops backed off and Stokely's Student Nonviolent Coordinating Committee (SNCC) went viral. He utilized the symbol of the Black Panther as his logo for his "Freedom Now Party." The Black Panther Party for Defense, organized by Huey Newton and Bobby Seale, regarded Martin, Malcolm, and Carmichael as direct influences. They galvanized the black movement throughout the United States as well as internationally.

Stokely continued his teaching by stressing that all African people are intertwined by fate. He stressed the need to remove any confusion about our identity by declaring that we are all African people. Stokely insisted that we needed to teach Pan-Africanism.

In discussions with my peers and the need for clarity in the newly instituted Black Study's Centers and departments, I thought it would be beneficial if we invited Stokely Carmichael to the UCLA campus to give a colloquium on Pan-Africanism. Ayuko Babu informed me that Stokely would not come to the West Coast because of a serious conflict he has with the Black Panther Party. However, he said, we are welcome to visit him and his revolutionary African wife, Miriam Makeba, in Washington, D.C. Miriam was denied reentry into South Africa, because of her anti-apartheid songs. She lived in exile for three decades and married Stokely in 1968.

The Director of the Asian Studies Center, Cynthia Ong, whose office was next to mine in Campbell Hall, helped me acquire the funding to fly my central committee, Ayuko Babu, Little Joe, Datari, and myself, to meet with Stokely and his wife in Washington, D.C. The meeting was very enlightening. We sat in a circle on his living room floor for two days discussing the core meaning of Pan-Africanism; grasping how the transatlantic slave trade scattered African people from their indigenous territories: and now the need to understand that "African people, both on the continent and in the diaspora, share, not merely a common history, but a common destiny."

Pan Africanism is based on the belief that the unity of people of African descent is vital to their economic, social, and political progress. The ideology asserts that the fate of all African people and countries are intertwined. I passed on the teachings to the other University campuses. Cal State Northridge was the first to respond back, indicating that they changed the name of their Black Study's Department to the "Pan African Studies Department".

The UCLA Philosophy Department invited me to become a member of their search committee. The Department was seeking to hire a Professor in Black Skin into their department. After examining many applications, we discovered a young female in black skin that was born in Alabama, studied French and philosophy in Germany, and received her doctorate at the University of Berlin. Her name was Dr. Angela Davis.

We flew her in for an interview and she left our committee simply awestruck. The process of hiring her began immediately. I received a phone call from Dr. Robert Singleton, the new Director of the African American Study

Center, at the beginning of my summer vacation, informing me that Angela was hired and coming to campus. He asked if I would come in and show her around campus and introduce her to the community. He stressed that it was important to get her adjusted ASAP, with the realization that I would be giving up my summertime with my family.

Meetings had been organized with the Black Alliance, Black Panther members and Ron Karenga's US organization in the inner city. I attended these meetings/discussions during that summer. In addition to her official class on campus, I opened up my home where she taught revolutionary classes to my central committee plus certain leaders from the black community including Black Professionals on campus like Professor Seneca Turner who was one of the teachers in the High Potential Program.

I served as her bodyguard on many other speaking engagements. In July Angela visited Cuba, and upon her return she showed me a one-page memo from UCLA's Chancellor, Dr. Charles E. Young. In her first communication with the Chancellor, he asked if she was a Communist.

Chancellor Young informed us that California Governor Ronald Reagan read in U.C. Berkeley's campus paper that "UCLA had just hired a communist." Now Governor Reagan wanted to invoke a 1949 regulation prohibiting the hiring of communists. Angela and I discussed the ramifications of admitting her party affiliations. She sent back at least two pages admitting in full disclosure her membership to the party.

From that moment on the Philosophy's Department process of hiring Angela was blocked. On October 3, 1969, three UCLA faculty members and I, as property owners, filed a taxpayers' lawsuit in the Superior Court of Los Angeles County against the Regents. We argued that "barring Angela Davis from employment because she was a member of the Communist Party was invalid under the First and Fourteenth Amendments to the Constitution of the United States and that the expenditure of tax monies in the implementation of such resolutions constituted an impermissible use of public funds.

Respondents; Kenneth L. Karst, David Kaplan, Douglas Glasgow, Webster Moore, Harry Deutsch, and Angela Y. Davis, Real-Parties in Interest." On October 20th Angela returned to campus and delivered her first lecture in Royce Hall.

On December 8th, 1969, I was awakened with a phone call around 5 A.M. from the Black Panther's Headquarters in Los Angeles. It was the secretary of the BSU, who was a member of the Black Panther Party. "We are surrounded by the police," she said. "They're shooting and they're going to dynamite the building. We're giving out of bullets and our gas cannisters are running out, we need help."

I jumped out of bed, called Angela, then went to the University and checked out some University Station Wagons. I then went to the dorms and alarmed the students in black skins. They jumped into the vehicles and headed for the Black Panthers' office in South Los Angeles. I wanted to stop the police from blowing up the building and killing our brothers and sisters.

What I learned later was that the police, without warning, broke into the Panthers' office with their guns out and were surprised when one Panther with a machine gun and another with a shotgun fired on them, forcing the cops out of their building. The cops dragged out one of their wounded and thus began the biggest Los Angeles shootout in American history.

The police had blocked off Central Avenue, but the area was full of students, local black politicians, and community people. Motorcycle cops kept patrolling the crowd of black faces witnessing the battle. A politician in black skin, tried to communicate with one of the motorcycle policemen by identifying himself as a local city Councilman. But the cop yelled at him:

"Shut Up, Nigger and get back!"

People in black skin watched from their buildings, and the streets were packed with black faces. I watched and wondered how we, united as people in black skins, could overtake the police force since our numbers were so much greater.

In the meantime, the cops were revving up their motorcycles, bullying the crowds of citizens in black skins when Angela suddenly looked at me and said this is crazy. "Let's go and get those kids out of there." We walked across the street, through the police line to their makeshift post.

We spoke to the officer in charge asking him for a cease-fire, and giving us a chance to talk to the Panthers about coming out before someone is killed. He agreed to disengage his armed forces and gave us permission to go tell the Panthers they could come out safely and wouldn't be shot.

The police stopped shooting and it was just she and I walking down the middle of the street toward the Panther headquarters. By the time we were almost there, they came out on their own, their cannisters had run out. One had been shot in the leg, otherwise all were alive and well. The officers didn't shoot them, as I'm sure they would have if Angela and I hadn't initiated that "Cease Fire," essentially allowing them to safely walk out. They were arrested, but they really won that four- to five-hour gun battle! Six panthers against over two hundred policemen, a small tank, and the newly formed Los Angeles SWAT team on their initial mission.

The following semester, 7 May 1970, members of the Ohio National Guard fatally shot four Ohio Kent State students in white skin, who were protesting our country's involvement in the Vietnam War. Our movement was in unison with their struggle. Malcolm X and Martin Luther King Jr. had made outspoken remarks against the Vietnam War. The BSU, the SDS, the Faculty and the Student Government came together in protest and literally closed down UCLA's campus. As a spokesman for the BSU, I became an integral part of the protest.

I met with Tom Hayden, leader of the Students for a Democratic Society (SDS), and a few other organizers. I was blown away by the amount of planning material SDS was sharing with us. They showed us a blueprint of escape routes, i.e., tunnels under the administration building. So, once we closed down the administration building, these were the escape routes available to the Chancellor and his administration.

Once our protestors, students, faculty, and staff occupied Murphy Hall, the administrative building, the Chancellor, in an unprecedented move, called in the Los Angeles Police Department to put an end to the student's campus wide protest. The UCLA campus paper reported that it was the "first time in campus history" that a UCLA Chancellor mobilized outside law enforcement to enter UCLA's campus to assault UCLA students and UCLA faculty.

The protest featured many speakers. I delivered a speech on the steps of Royce Hall, when the police swept across the UCLA campus swinging their batons and beating anyone in their path. I stayed inside the building out of site, because of the high visibility of Black Skin, until the campus was completely swept clean by the riot police. Hours later, when everything was quiet, I began walking across the campus from the Student Union Building, toward the office of the Black Student's Union in Campbell Hall where Angela and other members of the BSU were located. I quickly noticed a group of police officers in riot gear running full speed in my direction. I looked around and saw no other person in sight and I couldn't totally believe they were running that hard because of my lone figure. I tried to run out of their way, up some stairs by Royce Hall, and dash into a building out of their path. I wasn't fast enough because when I looked back over my right shoulder, a Billy-Club crashed into my head, right above the right eye socket. I was knocked off my feet, airborne until my body landed on the ground next to Royce Hall's Eastern wall. I was on my back, totally unconscious.

I noticed that I was literally outside of my body, I was above it! I felt no pain, but I could see and hear everything. The only movement I saw coming from my body was red blood gushing out of my face right above my right eye as it completely soaked my Dashiki. I watched as six officers leaned over me. I could see their facemasks in a circle around and over my body with their clubs cocked. I suddenly had the strange thought that this is the powerless position a woman experiences during a rape. The clubs of the six officers didn't crash down upon my skull. I was literally knocked out, lifeless. One cop reached down and felt my carotid artery. For a sign of life. And yelled, "He's alive, he'll be okay, let's drag him over the campus to set a good example for the rest of them." They knew exactly where my office was because they literally dragged me right past Campbell Hall and through its patio. I couldn't walk, but I heard black voices from the windows saying, "Look, they've got Webster."

When my family saw my swollen distorted face with eighteen stiches over my eyelid, my youngest daughter put her hands over her face and cried. It is ironic that this same daughter, 23 years later, was the Juror #7 that led the decision to convict two Los Angeles policemen for the relentless beating of Rodney King. King was another man in black skin beaten mercilessly by the police, but he wasn't knocked unconscious, he moved, so they beat him over and over and over again.

As in the case of Emmett Till, the nation was stunned when a video camera reached into the heart of Rodney King's beating and transmitted its naked repulsiveness into the homes of the nation. But, like Emmitt Teal, the policemen in white-skins were acquitted by an all-white-skinned-jury. This act ignited the inner-city citizens of Los Angeles to sack and burn down the city of Los Angeles. The anger ignited the flames in cities throughout the nation, forcing the President of the United States to stop business as usual and bring about a second trial. This time, that same young daughter that broke down in tears at the swollen distorted face of her father was now Juror #7, looking at the swollen distorted face of another male in black skin named Rodney King. This Juror educated the other eleven on exactly what they were looking at.

My daughter Maria-Helena, explained to me that the police officers continually met with the Jurors during their week of sequestration. She explained how the Jurors were made to look at the video of Rodney King over and over and over again, until the jurors became desensitized to the humanity of Rodney King. The police officers kept the jurors' focus on the body movements of Rodney King even though they had him handcuffed and laying down on the ground. The officers argued that their safety depended upon the arrestee's compliance, and each time they ordered him not to move he moved a muscle which meant that they had to hit him. Their training demanded that anything inconsistent with compliance is resistance, and resistance puts the officers' safety in danger.

After one month and 22 days of trial and sequestration, she was able to convince the other distressed jurors to see Rodney King as a handcuffed human being lying helplessly on the ground, being beaten relentlessly by four cops. Two of the officers were found guilty, and the inner-city citizens in black skins waiting to torch again, took a breath, the fires were not rekindled, and the city of Angels began repairing itself.

In the fallacious police report that summarized the motive for beating me into unconsciousness on the UCLA's campus was:

"He was throwing rocks and bottles, cursing at women and children, and resisting arrest."

After the doctors completed using 18 stiches to close up my head wounds, I was ordered into a courtroom in downtown Los Angeles to defend those charges. I obtained a public-defender and went to court every day for over a week to prove to the Judge that not only did I not commit any crime, but I was beaten by the police for simply walking across the lawn. It was simply unreal watching the public defender seriously arguing against the charges brought against me by the state's prosecutors every day for a week. Everyone involved knew that the whole procedure was a sham.

I had gotten behind on my classwork, so I had to focus upon maintaining my grade point average. I reduced my class load to a minimum of 12 units to remain a full-time student. The Educational Opportunity Program supplied me with a tutor in white skin to help me through the quarter. She was a tall thin blue-eyed blonde graduate student who was aware of my ordeal and she never missed nor was she ever late for any of my tutorial sessions. Toward the end of the quarter, before summer break, she asked what I was going to do during the break after such a horrendous beating, absurd trial and getting through all my classes. In an unrealistic tone and no forethought at all I said, "You know, after all I've encountered in this racist country, I want to go to my original home, I want to go to Africa!"

"Well," she said, "what's stopping you? I think it would be good for you."

I didn't have a quick answer for her. I thought only a white girl would think like that. "I don't hardly have the money," I said. "I can't just go to Africa for the summer." Without even a pause, or a change in tone, she simply said, "I have $3000.00 just sitting in the bank not doing anything. Take it, I think you really should go."

I discussed the budding trip with my wife. She thought that it was a fantastic opportunity that may never come again. My first thoughts on visiting Africa was the opportunity to meet up with Julius Nyerere, Tanzania's first President. Nyerere was a leading force in the Pan-African movement in East Africa as Kwame Nkrumah, noted as the father of Pan Africanism, was in West Africa. they both gave their lives in trying to unify Africa. Nyerere had also set up Tanzania as a training camp for liberation armies in South Africa, Southwest Africa and Zimbabwe. I was also interested in the Ujamaa cooperatives which Nyerere had organized. They were like the successful Kibbutz Cooperatives in Israel. So, I set my mind into leaving my frustrating encounters on college campuses and take this opportunity to join the real African struggle. I wanted to train in Tanzania and give my life for real freedom directly on the continent of Africa.

I packed my navy seabag, made sure my family was financially secure and completed all my goodbyes. My friend and fellow student Ayuko Babu drove me to studio-city to meet with Stevie Wonder in his studio. Stevie said he was sending some of his music into Tanzania and he was planning a tour through Africa, and he was particularly interested in connecting with President Nyerere and supporting the needs of the indigenous struggles in South Africa. He let us sit in during a practice session with his accompaniment before wishing me a successful journey.

The itinerary of the tickets I purchased flew me from Los Angeles to New York, New York to Paris, Paris to Egypt, Egypt to Nigeria, Nigeria to Congo Brazzaville, Congo to Tanzania.

I was really only interested in getting to Tanzania so the other stops, I thought, would only be a one- or two-day visit. I felt that most of my time, would be in Tanzania. Once I contacted Nyerere, I was hoping to get the training I needed to fight with the indigenous African people for freedom from the colonialism of South Africa.

I landed in Paris and immediately went to the Nigerian embassy to acquire my visa. The Nigerian embassy was completely staffed by Nigerians. Their jet-black skins attested to the statement that "Black is Beautiful." I went up to the desk and answered all their questions. The African gentleman behind the desk gave me a large welcoming smile. He grabbed my hand and started shaking it and explaining how wonderful Nigerian people are, especially his family in Lagos, the capital of Nigeria. When he discovered I hadn't made any hotel reservations, he came from around the desk and started telling me how I must meet his family. He went further stating that I must stay with them. I couldn't get in a word. He insisted that I stay with his relatives and proceeded to contact them. I explained that I had my sleeping bag and I stayed at a Hostel in Paris, and I would be okay. But no, he not only contacted them, but he said they would pick me up at the airport and since I was only staying one day in Lagos, I had to accept his hospitality.

There were no direct flights to Nigeria. My plane landed in Cairo, Egypt. Once I exited the plane going to get my baggage, I noticed that most of the passengers on the plane were in white skins. We were all in line to get our luggage when African Egyptian men in black skin were running to all the passengers in white skins asking obsequiously if they could carry their baggage, etc. They simply ignored me as well as other people in black skin. I picked up my sea-bag and sleeping-bag and walked around while waiting for the plane to Lagos, Nigeria.

I felt I was in a different time and place. I hadn't seen that kind of groveling toward whites not even in the South. It was sad to see. While waiting at the Cairo airport, I noticed these gigantic statues of men with full lips, wide noses, and facial structures like mine. They were called Pharaohs. I had never seen anything like it, not even in the movies. One was standing straight up, like a king. The others were sculpted right in the walls around the airport. I didn't have anyone to talk to and I wasn't going to ask these submissive acting Africans anything. But I had this funny feeling that I was looking at something outside of my sphere of knowledge and history. This was quite puzzling to me. However, I was experiencing so many puzzling episodes. After all, I was in a different country and I knew I had no knowledge of Egypt other than stories in the movies. So, I just headed for my plane since people were boarding.

CHAPTER X

NIGERIA

I landed in Lagos and as I disembarked, the Africans in black skins looking for tips by begging to carry people's bags ignored me as they did in Cairo. They only rushed to help those in white skins. However, a couple of Nigerians recognized me and actually called out my name. They took my hand, retrieved my bags, put me in a car and drove me out of the airport and into a village right outside the Capital.

I thought I would be in Nigeria for only one night. I ended up staying there a week. The next day the women took me to the marketplace where all the bartering was taking place for fresh colorful vegetables. The meats were freshly cut because there was no refrigeration. The men went into Lagos the Capital for work. When they came back, they came and got me. They held my hand as they walked through the village introducing me to their cousins, uncles, relatives, and friends. I had never walked down the streets with another man holding my hands. I knew they had no idea how uncomfortable I felt, but I knew I had to get over that because this was a purely different mindset, a different culture.

As we walked through the streets, I noticed there was a whole line of children following us. They were looking at me as if I were something extraordinary. I asked my hosts about it, and they said the children had never seen a black man with a beard, and I had come from a faraway land called America although I had originally been taken from their homeland.

My hosts continually insisted that my height and features were the same as theirs. They were taking me to meet my cousins because my features and theirs were clearly the same. About that time an old lady sitting on a porch signaled for them to bring me to her. I couldn't understand all of her words, but she made some gestures with her hands and then named me "Omowale." I asked for the meaning as we continued, and I was told it meant, "Son returned home."

One afternoon while I was sitting on a stomp leaning against a wall while watching the children in their traditional dress, while paying particular attention to their interaction with their peers and their elders.

I thought of myself at 8 years of age in my southern town of Mobile, Alabama. That was around 1945. I was living a similar existence in the sense that there was no such thing as juvenile delinquency. I remembered my Mom sending me to the local store with a few coins to buy her two cigarettes.

I watched the children playing with each other very innocently while noticing the young girls crossing the bridge leaving the villages and entering the Capital city of Lagos. They immediately perused the stores with lipstick, wigs, dresses, etc., . The villagers were used to bartering, they didn't have cash money to purchase these items. So right before my eyes I saw a couple of young girls coming back from downtown Lagos toward the village wearing miniskirts and lipstick.

Wow! What the young girls bartered to get the cash was different than that of their parents. The villagers had to go into town to find employment in order to have the needed exchange. Then I looked up and saw them building an overhead highway from the airport to the Capital. Here comes modernization, I thought. Here comes modernization with crime, prostitution, cars, gangs, and prisons. Poverty for many, riches for the few.

Another very subtle observance, there were no people in white skin. The feeling of living in a country and not seeing anyone in white skin was incredible. I don't think that there has ever been a day wherein the color of my skin weighed heavily on my mental and physical survival.

To have a life where you're daily struggling to be more than someone's property, knowing that because of the color of your skin, you will be treated differently according to what street you're on, what neighborhood, what city or state. Then find yourself among people who have never had the experience of subjugation based upon the color of their skin.

Your friends, peers, neighbors, government, parliament, President, shop owners, property owners, all are one people in black skin. It was a feeling that is exceedingly difficult to describe. A feeling of liberation that can only be understood by those who have lived in racial subjugation from birth.

Then there is the other side of the coin. The ethnicity of the family I lived with were Yoruba. They presided in the south-west of Nigeria. The Hausa in the North and the Ibo in the south-east. When I arrived, the country had just undergone a terrible Nigerian Civil War (^ July 1967- January 1970). I had not known about this when I arrived, so I was unbelievably speechless when I went walking alone toward the capital. There were dead bodies on the side of the road, not a few, but many, many dead bodies. People were walking by seemingly without any notice or concern. It was as if it was simply dead animals on the street. So, I acted as though I didn't notice also. There were simply so many questions, but I wasn't about to ask any since no one seem to notice. Not to mention that the people didn't speak English anyway. I later learned that the ethnic tensions were so intense that up to 30,000 Ibos were killed fighting the Hausas, and about 1 million refugees escaped to their homeland in the east.

It seemed that underneath the ethnic cleansing was the oil. Which ethnic group would be in charge to supply the industrialized countries their oil needs. It was insightful to learn how Israel, France, Britain and Russia supplied the weapons to their favorite ethnicity in order to solidify their cravings.

Finally, I had to say goodbye. When I left, it seemed like the whole village was at the airport to see me off. I really felt very humble and overwhelmed by their love, hospitality, and innocence. I flew out of Lagos. My visa was set for Congo Kinshasa, but to get into Kinshasa, I had to land in and travel through Congo Brazzaville, and then cross over on land to Kinshasa. However, when I landed in Brazzaville, they were undergoing an ethno-political civil war. In 1970, Mobutu, with the backing of the United States, had taken out Lumumba as the country's minister and had set up the Popular Movement of the Revolution. Patrice Lumumba brought in the country's first direct presidential election. It is interesting and significant to note that the Simba organization is the name adopted by the United States Ron Karenga's gang before they became the revolutionary US Organization.

The civil war between Mobutu and Lumumba was about which one of the leaders would partner with which industrialized country. So, Mobutu worked with the U.S. CIA to have Lumumba brutally beaten to death.

So, I arrived at the Congolese airport as this struggle was taking form. A group of militia men dressed in army combat uniforms, all carrying machine guns, escorted me from the plane onto the floor of the airport. I didn't speak their language but their direction using their machine guns as pointers made it clear that I had to keep quiet and sit on that floor all night under watch by two armed militiamen.

The next morning, they escorted me back to the airport and put me on a plane heading back to Lagos, Nigeria. They didn't speak any English, but an undercover operative was assigned to stay with me. I asked what was going on and he indicates that it was highly unusual for an American travelling alone with Visas through these African countries at this point in time made me look very suspicious. They decided to fly me back to Lagos, Nigeria. From Lagos I was to continue my itinerary to Tanzania and Kenya. On board the plane, the undercover watched my every move until I got off the plane back in Lagos.

I didn't want the Nigerian family nor anyone in the village I stayed in to know I was back in Lagos. I had to sleep on the benches at that airport until the next flight out the next morning for Tanzania.

TANZANIA

Humans are Homo Sapiens, a culture-bearing upright-walking species that lives on the ground and very likely first evolved in Africa about 315,000 years ago.

Russell Howard Tuttle

Tanzania's historic beginnings can be traced back to the first human beings that evolved on planet Earth. According to archeologist and paleoanthropologist Louis and Mary Leakey, following years of excavations, in 1959 they "discovered the near-perfect Skull of a man who inhabited an area often called "The Cradle of Mankind." The "near-perfect Skull" was found to be between 2.3 and 1.2 million years old and the "Cradle of Mankind" is now called Tanzania, *(Encyclopedia Britannica)*

In the early 1800, traders would enter this "Cradle" from the island of Zanzibar. The actual word Tanzania was a combination of the word "Tanga" meaning "sail" and Zanzi ("Zenj") which is a local name meaning black, and "Barr" meaning coastal area. The country also houses the highest mountain in Africa, Mount Kilimanjaro, and borders the longest freshwater lake in the world, Lake Tanganyika.

The country gained its independence from Britain in 1961. However, the historical European colonization left the population with land and animals, but no manageable system of cultivation needed to build a livable economy. The indigenous population was forced to import food to prevent hunger and malnutrition. They began migrating from rural areas into urban areas for employment.

IN 1954, Julius Nyerere was one of two Tanganyika's who completed his higher education degrees like Kwame Nkrumah, Martin Luther King Jr., Malcolm X, Ron Karenga, Huey Newton, like Angela Davis, and an untold number of trailblazers who acquired higher education degrees before grasping the momentous leadership roles in their respective organizations, communities, and countries. After Nyerere received his master's degree he became a school teacher: organized the Tanganyika Africa Union (TANU), entered the Legislative Council, and became the Chief Minister in 1960. In 1961 he became the first Prime Minister and facilitated Tanzania's attainment of full independence in 1962. In 1964 his leadership resulted in the creation of the Republic of Tanzania where he was elected Tanzania's first president. He wrote and implemented "The Arusha Declaration" in 1967 which was Tanzania's most prominent political statement of African co-operatives, also referred to as "Ujamaa" or "Brotherhoods." Self-Reliance stood out as the most important part of the declaration with his understanding that "a poor man does not use Money as a weapon:"

> We have chosen the wrong weapon for our struggle because we chose money as our weapon. We are trying to overcome our economic weakness by using the weapons of the economically strong – weapons which in fact we do not possess. By our thoughts, words, and actions, it appears as if we have come to the conclusion that without money, we cannot bring about the revolution we are aiming at. It is as if we have said, "Money is the basis of development. Without money, there can be no development"

...The development of a country is brought about by people, not by money. Money, and the wealth it represents, is the result and not the basis of development." In addition to people, the prerequisites of development are land, good policies and good leadership and the necessary condition and root of development are the hard work and intelligence of the people.

(Publicity Section, TANU, Dar es Salaam, 1967, p. 5).

My purpose for visiting Tanzania was to observe the operation of their Agricultural Co-operatives and Ujamaa villages along with the Kibbutz co-operatives in Israel which, I toured before returning to the United States. Another reason for being in Tanzania was my unrevealed desire to join the military struggle in Southern Africa since President Nyerere's government provided training and aid to anti-colonialist groups fighting white-minority rule throughout Southern Africa. That aid included military training.

I was introduced to leaders of Nyerere's military training schools who took me to one of their training grounds wherein they convinced me that there wasn't the slightest need for my joining the physical struggle when they had an unlimited supply of bodies, also I would have to deal with the languages. However, they expressed an important service by providing their fighters with military boots and medical supplies. I witnessed the Africans doing military training barefooted. I promised that I would return to the United States and send back Military Boots and Medical Supplies.

The first thing on my agenda after returning to the University of California at Los Angeles, was to have the Black Student's Union put together a campaign to fund and send a thousand military boots and medical supplies in order to fulfill that promise. We ended up having an amazing Jazz benefit on UCLA's campus when the renowned Jazz Saxophonist Pharoah Sanders, agreed to be the headliner. We flew him in where he and his fellow musicians entertained the Westwood campus for two straight nights.

The student's response was overwhelming. The concert was sold out immediately. We sold over a thousand tickets which provided the funds to send over a thousand military boots and Medical Supplies directly to President Nyerere as promised.

CARNEGIE ENDOWMENT FOR INTERNATIONAL PEACE

When I returned from Tanzania, I submitted a paper on my travels in Africa which completed my degree requirements. I was now a University of California Graduate majoring in Political Science, with a consecration in International Relations. My dream goal, as a Political Science graduate, was to become a Foreign Service Officer (FSO). So, when UCLA's Political Science Department nominated me for a Fellowship with "CARNEGIE ENDOWMENT FOR INTERNATIONAL PEACE," I was honored, but when "CARNEGIE" accepted me as one of their Fellows to do research at the United Nations, I was speechless. Each year Carnegie Endowment offers approximately 14 one-year fellowships to uniquely qualified graduating seniors and individuals who have graduated during the past academic year. The graduates are selected from a pool of nominees nominated by several hundred participating universities and colleges. Carnegie Fellows work as research assistants with Carnegie's senior scholars.

Carnegie Endowment for International Peace is a nonpartisan international affairs think tank headquartered in Washington D.C. with operations in Europe, South and East Asia, and the Middle East. The organization describes itself as being dedicated to advancing cooperation between countries, reducing global conflict, and promoting active international engagement with countries around the world. It aspires to be the first global think tank, the place that brings what the world thinks into thinking about U.S. policy and to communicate that thinking back to a global audience.

Now, in 1971, the world was thinking about the underlying reason that caused the United States of America to completely flip its foreign policy and use its Superpower Veto for the 1st time in history, against the United Nations and the participating global community to stop mandatory sanctions against a country in Southern Africa named Rhodesia. Carnegie brought its chosen graduates to Washington D.C. to investigate and communicate the resulting thinking back to its global audience.

Miriam Makeba at the U.N. 1964

Rhodesia was a self-governing British colony in Southern Africa where 200,000 Rhodesians in white skin ruled over 4 million Rhodesians of black skin which institutionalized a system of racial segregation called Apartheid. In the fall of 1965, Time magazine commented that "Few communities in the world can match the sundrenched affluence that Rhodesia's hardy settlers have achieved for themselves." The United Nations was gaining momentum toward ending apartheid in its member nations that were rising in armed resistance to the rule of the ruthless white minority regime throughout southern Africa. The Civil Rights activist and renowned singer Miriam Makeba, born in South Africa, testified in 1964 before the United Nations, exposing the racial policies of a minority of citizens in white skins using their military advantage to dominate politically, socially, and economically, the majority of citizens in Black Skin. In late 1966, Britain decided to take the lead against its Rhodesian Colony by refusing to grant the Colony's independence until it worked out a plan for majority rule.

When Rhodesia's Prime Minister, Ian Smith, refused to engage in a plan toward majority rule, Britain made the historic move to lead the other United Nations to impose economic sanctions against Rhodesia. This was historic because it was the first time the United Nations had ever imposed mandatory sanctions. The United Sates was totally in agreement with Britain and the rest of the United Nations until 1971.

In 1971, The White House, under President Nixon, used its Superpower Veto to stop the mandatory sanctions. Thus, demonstrating its indifference toward its former agreement with Britain and the cause of the majority of Rhodesians in black skins, as well as a blatant indifference toward the global community.

Carnegie Endowment for International Peace 4 top graduates from Universities and Colleges across the United States arrived at the Capital to meticulously investigate and publish the underlying reason that caused the U.S. to flip its foreign policy.

I was now a Carnegie Fellow assigned as a research assistant for the special assistant to the president for U.S. National Security, Dr. Anthony Lake. Anthony had previously served as a Foreign Service Officer for 9 years. He proceeded in providing a roadmap for my stay in the Capital including the contact information needed to set-up my interviews with members of the United Nations involved in the policy, senators, and officials with information pertinent to the study.

The most important interview I experienced was with a former member of the original "White House Fellows Program" created in 1965, later continued as the Carnegie Endowment for International Peace. I had no idea at the time whom this towering man in black skin was named General Colin Powell. I shared with him U.N. documents supporting the 1971 Byrd amendment which enabled the United States to import chromite ore from Rhodesia favoring a private corporation, "Foothill Minerals," that owned the Chromite mine in Rhodesia. Senator Byrd lobbied the President of the U.S. to tell the United Nations and the global community that it was necessary for National Security reasons. However, the research revealed that the National Security of the United States was not threatened. The information given to veto the Mandatory Sanctions was false.

Webster, you have to understand that our personal feelings, our personal knowledge, and what's right and what's wrong aren't part of our job description. We are senior executive employees who are advisors and conduct negotiations relating to foreign affairs, but we are given speeches that are written for us to deliver. Our job is to follow orders and deliver the message/s and or speeches we've been given. Our position dictates the urgency, power, and sincerity necessary since it has been mandated by the President of the United States. You must know that President Nixon doesn't know anything about Rhodesia, he couldn't find it on a map. You know Webster, we're really just secretaries. Powerful Corporations owning resources in other countries inform the President of their economic needs, thus affecting our foreign policy decisions.

When I returned to Carnegies office, I passed on the taped interview and my thinking about U.S. policy in concert with the other Fellows. Carnegie's senior scholars would compile and communicate that thinking back to the global audience.

Dr. Anthony Lake, my senior scholar, came over and asked how I was doing. I shared how I was really appreciating the opportunity and how I loved doing research. He shared how he appreciated my focus, dedication, and social skills. He asked about my future goals. I quickly shared that after this Fellowship, I wanted to get a position with the United Nations, I wanted to be a Foreign Service Officer. He hesitated, moved closer to me and said softly, "Well you know, Webster, when you get back to UCLA, you need to change your major. I'm just telling you this on the side, but the CIA [Centra Intelligence Agency] has your name. They've got you down as working with Angela Davis, and so you'll never be able to get a position in Washington in political science." (Webster E Moore, p48)

CHAPTER XI

Cal State University Northridge

After graduating from UCLA and completing Carnegie's Fellowship, I accepted a position at Cal State University Northridge as the Director of the Umoja Tutorial Center. Umoja is a Swahili word meaning unity. Unity is the first of the seven principles of Kwanzaa, an annual African American holiday (December 26-January 1), founded by Maulana Karenga. CSUN's Umoja Tutorial Center, Pan African Studies Department, and the Educational Opportunity Program were all results from the Civil Rights Movements of the late 1960s. Students in black skins throughout the nation demanded the hiring of faculty and recruitment of students in black skins.

Cal State University Northridge (CSUN) is unique since it became one of the first universities in the nation to establish a Black Studies Department, rather than a Black Studies Program. The Department is an administrative unit composed of its own faculty, curriculum, and G.E. requirements.

The department's name changed from Black Studies to African American Studies to Pan-African Studies. These changes reflect the changes in the consciousness of the students, faculty, and staff. They reflected on the self-consciousness movement of communities in black skin throughout the United States. Stokely Carmichael stands out as one good example of change. He was born in Trinidad, educated at

Howard University, and married to the renowned South African singer and activist, Miriam Makeba. He organized the global Pan-African movement, the Student Non-Violent Coordinating Committee, and became the "Honorary Prime Minister of the Black Panther Party."

In 1968, the first Educational Opportunity Program (EOP) was established at CSUN. It included the Umoja Tutorial Center, a Counseling Center, and a Tutorial Center. Despite the support in the PAS Department, Counseling, and Tutorial Center, still over 50% of enrolled students in black skins never made it to their junior year. The regular university faculty had little concern about the high dropout rate. The campus data revealed that 32% of regularly admitted students in white skin dropped out equally if not more than students of color. The loss of millions of students through attrition over the years had not captured any meaningful concern from the CSU system because their faculty's tenure was not based on how many students dropped out, but only on how many were enrolled. There was nothing in the formula that rewarded the faculty for performance, whether students graduate or not.

There was and still is a real drop in the number of students in white skin enrolling. The demographic changes reveal the reduced need for families in white skins to have lots of children. The decline in enrollment means a decline in faculty positions. A decline in faculty positions means a decline in class sizes which means a decline in building funds. This was also having an effect in the community. The white community high schools first noticed a drop in students and were preparing to lay off teachers in the white Northridge community. They alleviated the problem by bussing in students from the black and brown communities. Suddenly, the classes were again full by bussing in thousands of students of color thus, saving the jobs of the white faculty. The recruitment arm of the Educational Opportunity Program no longer had to leave CSUN and travel into the inner city to bring in students of color. Now they were being bussed into the local former white community schools.

The need to stabilize the academic system had turned the literature concerning education into a comparative analysis of the demographic and academic characteristics of students in black skin,. Brown-skins, yellow-skins, and white-skins. The data being published pointed to the waste of EOP funds spent on students in black skins because their dropout rate was statistically higher than all students on the campus. Troubled by such a publication coming from our university. I immediately contacted the Office of Student Affairs and had them rerun those statistics and look at the students according to their zip codes rather than skin color. The results clearly indicated that the high number of dropouts was significantly dependent upon Social-Economic Conditions, not the color of one's skin!

While working with the Pan African Studies faculty in reducing student retention, and recognizing the demographic changes in the university, faculty member Vern Bryant and I decided to elevate the EOP recruitment and retention tools to the position of a recruitment and retention program not just for EOP students, but for the total university.

MALIBU FIRE AND NORTHRIDGE EARTHQUAKE

Around noon on November 2, 1993, someone shouted to me that the city of Malibu, where I lived, was on fire. I thought it was a joke, but it wasn't. The firestorm consumed everything I owned except the clothes I was wearing and the pickup I was driving. The Governor of California declared a state of emergency and "The Federal Management Agency (FEMA) responded to the losses and set me up in a new apartment in Calabasas, a city eight miles from Cal State Northridge.

I was just adjusting to this new neighborhood in November 1993 when I received an emergency call and had to rush my youngest brother to the hospital where he died due to a liver condition. After his death, our family spent a sobering Christmas together. A Christmas that felt empty without his physical presence. I pushed through that holiday and tried to look forward to the beginning of a new year in my new apartment in Calabasas.

I was awakened around 4:30 am that January of 1994 when the bed I was in started rolling like I was in a boat. After a few minutes, I made it out of the building and noticed the cracks in the building and the extreme damage throughout the whole complex. I had survived a 6.7

magnitude earthquake that shook the surrounding area for up to 30 miles for 10 seconds. The quake's activity was felt as far away as Las Vegas and San Diego. I was informed that my place of work, California State University Northridge was completely closed down for the whole Fall semester. I moved to Los Angeles to stay with my mother because her home was within walking distance from my classes at U.S.C.

The next day I drove into the Northridge campus to assess any damages to my office and to retrieve any needed materials. I noticed many empty buildings including an empty house on campus that didn't seem as though it was in use even before the earthquake. I contacted building management and found out there weren't any plans at that time on record for the building. I used my official position as the advisor to the Black Students Union on campus with a serious need for students in black skin to have a home on campus, a supportive place, especially after the earthquake where many will need this house that's not being utilized. The officials in charge saw this is a positive utilization of the building and signed the building over to **the" Black House,"** under Cal State University's Black Student's Union.

The next day I remember sort of being in a mentally foggy state sitting on Mom's porch and reading a letter addressed to me from the State Chancellors' Office.

Dear Mr. Webster E Moore

On your birthdate, you will have reached the age of 55. This date will also be your 20th year with the California State University System. We are happy to inform you that this year we are offering the "Golden Handshake" to employees that may desire to take early retirement. The offer would allow you to receive the same amount of monetary benefits that you would receive at age 60. This offer will only be available to you this birth date, it will not be available after this.

That was like a letter from heaven to me. I took the "Golden Handshake."

CHAPTER XII

RODNEY KING

On the early morning of March 2, 1991, three Los Angeles police officers were caught on a video kicking, stomping, and beating a man in black skin named Rodney King with a metal baton.

An all-white jury acquitted the officers. Once that verdict hit the streets, the worst civil rebellion of the century exploded in Los Angeles. The city was torched, freeways were blocked, white motorists were beaten. I drove down the streets watching businesses go up in smoke, uncontrollable looting in every direction. Over 7,000 people were arrested, hundreds of millions of dollars' worth of property destroyed. President George Bush and Attorney General William Barr addressed the nation and began the processes of a 2nd trial leading to the prosecution of the officers in order to quell the rage.

I was totally shocked to learn that Maria-Helena, my youngest daughter, living in Orange County, was selected as a juror in this historic federal trial of the four officers. It seems that she was chosen as a Juror because, in questioning potential Jurors, she was found to be practically oblivious to the beating of Rodney King as well as the heated events surrounding the Los Angeles rebellion. My daughter's husband had been killed in an automobile accident as he was driving to pick her up from work. She was still in mourning during that period. She was also surrounded by her Orange County community of white skins which kept her isolated from the anger and chaos experienced by the inner- city community of black-skin citizens. Maria's apolitical persona and her unblack name helped secure her a position on the Jury even though the defense lawyers worked hard to keep potential jurors with black skin frombeing selected.

After undergoing "one month & twenty-two" tense days locked in a room in downtown Los Angeles, she called me stating she was afraid that the police or someone in the conservative atmosphere of Orange County where she lived, might cause harm to her since she was pushing the jurors toward a conviction. The tension among the jurors had reached such a high pitch that the one other black-juror's skin broke out in hives—so he left. Helen's experience—seeing my swollen head in the hospital after being beaten by police—allowed her to stay focused upon the humanity in Rodney King, which she used to lead the other jurors to a conviction of two of the officers. Thus, discharging the pent-up emotions of the Los Angeles community.

When Helen called me, I was enrolled in a doctorial program at the University of Southern California. However, I felt her fears at the time outweighed my class load. I dropped the class and drove downtown and then to her home in Orange County to be with her doing the media attention, interviews, and fatigue.

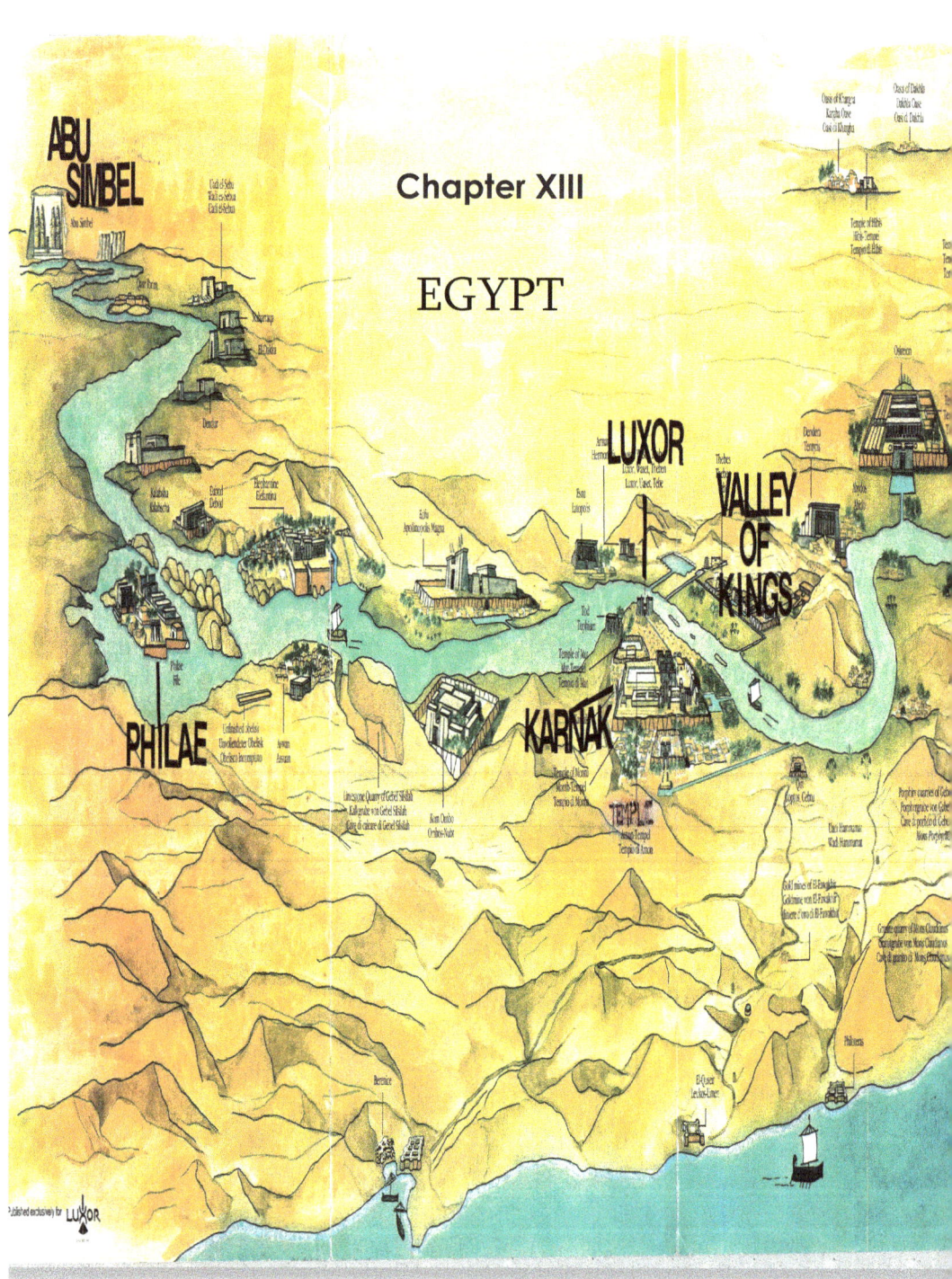

Chapter XIII

EGYPT

THE GREAT SPHINX

After I settled down from the exhilaration of my Nubian brothers linking my features to the Pharaoh Ramsey II, I was now open and fully prepped for my second escapade, visiting the only surviving structure among the seven wonders of the world, the Great Pyramid of Giza.

However, before I could get close to that wonder, I had to face an enormous sculpture, 241 feet long and 65 feet high, guarding the causeway leading to the Great Pyramid of Giza. This great sculpture was carved out of a single piece of stone, universalizing it as the most immense stone sculpture ever made by man. It also remains to this day, the oldest known religious monument in history denoting both body and soul.

The Great Sphinx depicts the human head of a Pharaoh and the lower body of a lion. It is considered religious because it's head, with the Cobra sculptured around its forehead - called the Uraeus, represented

divine knowledge or intelligence, while the animal body below represented the form, the physical vehicle that housed that divine intelligence. This picture illustrates the cobra on forehead. It's important to keep in mind that the soul, the spirit, the Christ, were the identifiers for divine intelligence.

When I think of divine intelligence as the power of a great artist, a sculpturist working through me, I remembered the words written by Thomas Troward in "The Power in You:"

> *the distinctive power of spirit is thought*
> *and*
> *the distinctive power of thought is form*

So, this massive sculpture, this form, this Sphinx, emerged from the thought of the spirit of our ancestors. As I stood transfixed on trying to contemplate the lesson of the Sphinx. I had to center myself so as not to be overwhelmed by size, the headpiece, the snake that was around the forehead but had been broken or worn off, the gigantic paws, the length of the lion's body, the sculptured tail, and why was it built before the pyramids? Finally, I focused upon the human head atop the body of a lion.

I thought of the power within me. Who I am compared to others who only see and define me according to the color of my skin, whether I have a tail, the size of my brain, the size of my lips, whether my hair is kinky or straight, and the size of my buttocks. The head atop the body clearly represent spirit, intelligence, livingness. The lesson of the Sphinx is not to be defined by others, but "knowing thyself." The significance of knowing that the spirit is the essential living being of the body. The realization and understanding that there is no life without spirit and there is no motion without body. However, the being must be able to realize its own will power in order to control motion which demonstrate its ingrained intelligence.

The fantastic granite monuments we're about to experience, are projections of the thoughts of these great minds. I've discovered this knowledge to be the keystone, the foundation of the religion or better the spirituality of Egypt. It is the mystical linkage I was feeling when I found myself surrounded by these magnificent monuments. The feeling of oneness is none other than feeling the spirit within because the spirit is not limited by the body. This is the most salient point to lock-in. The spirit does not take up space nor time. The body does. The spirit actually exists everywhere in the here and now. It is omnipresent.

Gerald Massey, the renowned Egyptologist, poet, and author on spiritualism and Ancient Egypt, inscribed on his epigraph:

"Born 1828, Re-born 1907."

That epigraph, I thought, encapsulated his conceptualization of not only the spiritual principle that propagated the first documented civilization, but it embodied our ancient ancestor's message of the Immortality of our very life. The embodiment of the cycles of birth and rebirth.

Statue of Osiris
Ptolemaic Period, 332-330 B.C.

A large statue of Osiris from the Late Period was placed in a niche of the crypt to create the impression of an open naos. The eyes, inlaid with white stone and black glass, give the god a striking expression. His body is made from wood and would originally have been wrapped with like a mummy in linen stiffened with plaster. The plumes, ram's horns, and uraeus (a cobra with its hood extended), are in bronze, as are the two scepters-the crook and flail-he holds in each hand. Osiris, the great national god of the dead, was adopted throughout the entire land and worshipped in many temples during the later periods of ancient Egypt

They understood that though they were born in physical bodies, their Pharaohs, their temples, their sculptures, their architecture all contained an immortal divine power within. They watched the annual birth, death, and rebirth of vegetation. The perpetual rising of the sun in the east, reaching its maturity, and then falling beneath the earth only to rise again. They literally built their temples on the eastern side of the Nile River where the sun rises and buried their dead beneath the earth on the west side of the Nile so their souls would rise from the dead with the sun as it rose daily in the east.

Life is spiritual and returning to the source was not only the aim for the Pharaohs, but it was the teaching, preparation, and purpose of the whole society. The coming of their first Pharaoh and great teacher Ausar, who was killed, became enlightened, and resurrected, established the belief that any Egyptian could survive his death if only he lived and died according to the principles of Justice which they called MAAT.

The 42 Laws of Maat: The Original Commandments?

Cornerstone of knowledge

1- I have not committed sin

2- I have not committed robbery with violence

3- I have not stolen

4- I have not slain men and women

5- I have not stolen food

6- I have not swindled offerings

7- I have not stolen from God

8- I have not told lies

9- I have not carried away food

10- I have not cursed

11- I have not closed my ears to truth

12- I have not committed adultery

13- I have not made anyone cry

14- I have not felt sorrow without reason

15- I have not assaulted anyone

16- I am not deceitful

17- I have not stolen anyone's land

18- I have not been an eavesdropper

19- I have not falsely accused anyone

20- I have not been angry without reason

21- I have not seduced anyone's wife

22- I have not polluted myself

23- I have not terrorized anyone

24- I have not disobeyed the law

25- I have not been excessively angry

26- I have not cursed God

27- I have not behaved with violence

28- I have not caused disruption of peace

29- I have not acted hastily or without thought

30- I have not overstepped my boundaries of concern

31- I have not exaggerated my words when speaking

32- I have not worked evil

33- I have not used evil thoughts, words or deeds

34- I have not polluted the water

35- I have not spoken angrily or arrogantly

36- I have not cursed anyone in thought, word or deed

37- I have not placed myself on a pedestal

38- I have not stolen that which belongs to God

39- I have not stolen from or disrespected the deceased 40- I have not taken food from a child

41- I have not acted with insolence

42- I have not destroyed property belonging to God

Many people have read or at least heard the biblical story of Moses and the Ten Commandments. What I find interesting is so many know about the 10 commandments but have never heard of the 42 Laws of Maat. Maat was the Egyptian Goddess designed to avert chaos and maintain truth (Maat) in ancient Kemet (Egypt).

This Egyptian Spirituality became the rock, the foundation, the stability, the discipline, the order the society lived by. It was through Maat, representing divine law, that order was achieved, thus allowing Civilization to blossom for over three-thousand years. This belief became so incredibly popular that it infused the culture and assimilated a central belief in a life after death and the belief in living perpetually.

PHYSICAL FEATURES

I couldn't help noticing that the nose of the Great Sphinx was chiseled off alone with the Uraeus. The Uraeus is a cobra snake sculpted on the forehead to symbolize the divine authority over the animal or human body.

When Napoleon Bonaparte arrived in Egypt in the 18th century the body of this Great Sphinx was completely buried in the desert sand. Only its head was protruding such that the rumor spread that his army used the Sphinx's facial features for target practice. However, an Arab historian documented that the Sphinx's nose was missing before

Napoleon's venture and a Sheikh called Mohamed Saaem el-Dahr eliminated the nose. It wasn't until the late 1930s that sand was finally removed from the Sphinx's body, freeing the total sculpture from its sandy tomb.

There was an ongoing dialogue about the number of sculptures with their noses missing or seemingly chiseled off, too many to be coincidental. The discussions centered around the enormous amount of energy involved in climbing upon these amazing wonders for the purpose of removing any evidence that these African Pharaohs were African people. We have all grown up in a culture that teaches us that there were never any Pharaohs in Black Skin. That the Pharaohs were white people or a mixture of white and red people. This reminds me of an incident in

Los Angeles, California, when I went to see an exhibit at the Museum on Wilshire Blvd. It was a tour of King Tutankhamun's royal tomb at the La brea's Tar Pits. I was so excited for the opportunity to see his actual sarcophagus and Golden Mask being brought out of Africa to a location a few miles from my home. I was literally taken aback— when I looked at King Tut's face on a 3ft-by-4ft illustration leading into the event.; They had printed his skin color pink. I couldn't believe that portrayal. This picture on the right is a copy from the tomb of Tutankhamun. The realization that the boy king's skin color was really black the unacceptable reality!

In Ivan Van Sertima's Book "EGYPT REVISITED:"

"..given Tutankhamen's immediate and distant ancestors, his surviving mummy and the valuable relics that depict his facial features, one cannot escape the conclusion that...The features of this Egyptian King, whose mother was of pure black stock, are almost as Negroid as the ones of his captured Nubian enemies.p283

2King Tut's Grandmother, Queen Tire

Pharaoah King Tutankhamen

Pharaonic History Prior to Egypt

It became noticeably clear that I had to better understand my ancestral history. Thanks to the internet I discovered some incredible research from a monumental excavation in southern Egypt from 1960-1964, a decade before my visit. The excavation uncovered evidence of Megalithic structures built over 11,000 years ago, but evenmore significantly, they found the first-ever recordings of Africans in black skins practicing astronomy. These findings document a stage of systematic development used to build an advanced culture. This signifies unearthing the very first Scientists ever discovered in human history! Dr. Bruce Williams, under the auspices of UNESCO, published 7 volumes of data substantiating these findings in the Nubian desert.

I correlated this research with a New York Times headline in 1979 which read: "Evidence of the oldest recognizable monarchy in human history, preceding the rise of the earliest Egyptian kings by several generations, has been discovered in artifacts from ancient Nubia." The article estimated that "The first kings of Ta-Seti *(Upper Egypt)* may well have ruled about 5900 B.C." An Archeology Magazine cited further that Dr. Bruce Williams, University of Chicago, "unveiled a birthplace of pharaonic civilization several generations before the rise of the first historic Egyptian dynasty." Ivan Van Sertima, associate professor of Africana Studies at Rutgers University in the U.S. reported that palaces, hieroglyphs, and the falcon deity Heru, was uncovered. All found thousands of years later in Kemet (Egypt).

The Egyptian Kingdoms

In fact, archaeological evidence suggests that humans had developed settled societies along the Nile River as early as 6,000 BCE. These people formed several kingdoms that, while they shared cultural traits, they were nevertheless independent kingdoms. Archaeological findings continually document Homo-Sapiens in black skins bringing civilization down the Nile "over 11,000 years BCE."

According to Edward Malkowski, ANCIENT EGYPT 39,000 BCE p62, an African Pharaoh by the name of Narmer (or Menes) is documented as uniting Upper and Lower Egypt around 3000 BCE. His African features are evident in the stone head carving. This Pharaoh is documented as the Pharaoh of the 1st Dynasty according to the

Egyptian Manetho, who wrote the first history of the Egyptians in the 1st century A.D., "including the ancient Egyptian's Kings list. a history that reaches forty thousand years into the past." (Malkowski p247)

Narmer 1st Pharaoh c.3150-2613 BCE

The Palermo Stone is one of seven large stone fragments with inscribed records of the ancient list of Pharaohs in black skins of ancient Egypt from the first to the fifth dynasty, i.e., from 2925 BCE. 2325 This chronological list of kings represents one of the basic sources

of information about the cultural history of ancient Egypt during the first five dynasties. The Stone also chronicles an earlier African *c i v i l i z a t i o n between twenty and thirty thousand years prior to the present one.* This civilization dates back between twenty and thirty thousand years

The king List of the main portion of the Palermo Stone preserved at Palermo, Sicily

before 2925 BCE. This research is not only documented on these Stones, but they have been corroborated.

In summary, there's an engrained xenophobic culture that has besieged western civilization to such an extent that true African history has been completely eliminated from the educational institutions throughout the United States of America. The African people in black skins who flourished for thousands of years before civilization reached the shores of Greece or Rome has been unthinkable in the academic academies of America. Thousands of years of true black history has been related to 400 years of U.S. slave history. The names and achievements of years of our Pharaonic Ancestors are simply not taught.

Professor George James in "Stolen Legacy," captured my attention when he wrote about mental slavery and how it affects the mind of people. I remember Kwame Nkrumah, who lead Africa to its first independent country, Ghana, raising such an awareness in his book on "Consciencism." The revolutionary freedom fighter, Malcolm X also taught extensively on this subject. All three made similar descriptions about how the person who is in mental bondage are "self-contained." "Not only will that person fail to challenge beliefs and patterns of thought virtually with her las dying effort.

The Professor continued raising my awareness by citing the centuries which the world was misled by falsely teaching that Socrates, Plato and Aristotle were the authors of Greek Philosophy without illustrating the fact that they were undesirable citizens constantly undergoing relentless persecutions by the Athenian Government:

Anaxagoras was imprisoned and exiled; Socrates was executed; Plato was sold into slavery and Aristotle was indicted and exiled; while the earliest of them all, Pythagoras, was expelled from Croton in Italy. (Stolen Legacy, p3)

The overwhelming evidence leads us to the conclusion that "Greek philosophers were not the authors of Greek philosophy, but the Egyptian Priests and Hierophants." "From the sixth century B.C....to the death of Aristotle (322 B..) the Greeks learned all they could about the Egyptian culture; most students received instructions directly from Egyptian Priests, but after the invasion by Alexander the Greek, the Royal Temples and libraries were plundered and pillaged, and

Aristotle's school converted the library at Alexandria into a research centre. There is no wonder then, that the production of the unusually large number of books ascribed to Aristotle has proved a physical impossibility, for any single man within a life time."

THE AFRICAN PYRAMIDS OF GIZA

While walking from the Sphinx toward the Great Pyramid of Giza, I thought that I would climb to the top of that great monument as soon as I touched its foundation. However, the magnitude of the Pyramid was too overwhelming. The average stone that I placed my hands upon weighed about 16 tons each. This isn't even realizing that the foundational stones which my feet were standing on must have weighed over 1600 tons each. The records indicate the pyramid not only consisted of 2.3 million blocks of stone, but it was so architecturally structured that it remained the tallest man-made structure in the world for over 3,800 years. The thought of climbing up to its zenith completely vanished from my mind as soon as my hands met the first stone. The feeling I had, standing at the foot of this colossal wonder, simply humbled me. I felt I had to take what could be a once-in-a-lifetime opportunity to go into its inner chamber, so I was directed to enter the Great Pyramid through the "robber's tunnel." I had to literally crawl into an ascending passageway 129 feet long. Then I entered the King's Chamber.

The floor, walls and ceiling of the chamber were made from rose granite. This specific granite was found to have been brought in from the Great Lakes area in central Africa, the same area that the 1st wood pyramids were built; the country is called the Sudan today. The ceiling was one complete stone that weighed about 600 tons alone. I walked over to an empty rose-granite sarcophagus in the center of this king's chamber and put my hands on the stone in order to sense its energy.

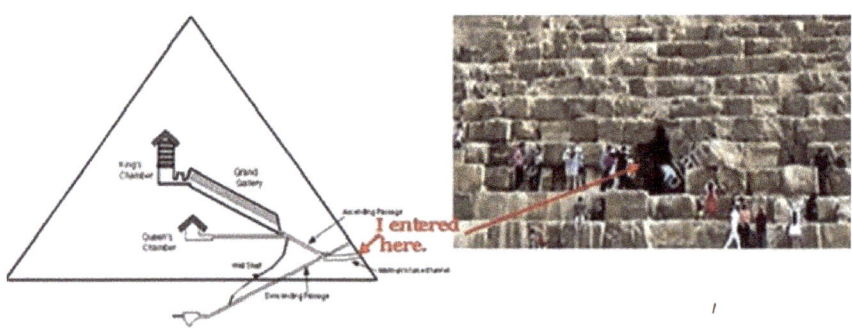

MUMMIFICATION

After leaving the Pyramids I was guided to a stone structure wherein the ancient Egyptians mummified their dead. Our tour guide, a professor from Cairo's public University, explained to us that no other civilization has ever devoted more of its resources and energy to preparing for immortality than the Egyptians. Whereas death in our western culture, is looked upon with intense fear, horror and sadness, the ancient Egyptians, saw death as a passageway to eternal life.

Ausar (Osiris), the pre-historic deified leader that led them into such an advanced stage of development, was killed, and resurrected to guide their souls into the afterlife.

The ancient Egyptians so identified with Ausar and his resurrection, that I noticed many of their prayers on the temple walls and sarcophaguses began with the term "Anuk–Ausar," meaning "*I am*

Ausar." That saying brought to mind the Christian's sayings, *"In the name of Jesus, etc."* The Ancient Egyptians believed they could only get into the afterlife or heaven by identifying with the oneness of God, the oneness of Ausar.

The ancient Egyptians were resurrectionists. However, in the latter dynasties, their priests decided to perfect a way to reuse their physical bodies to serve them again in the afterlife as they did in their present life. This was the beginning of the process of Mummification. So, the need to keep their bodies from decaying became paramount. They removed all the organs, except the heart, from the body to keep the body from decaying. They then dehydrated the body so it was preserved and could reanimate in the next world. This was the process of mummification.

Our tour guide shared an interesting concept. He said that the Egyptian Priests knew that the day would come when our "modern" race would perfect the process of cloning. Once any parts of their body are cloned, the Pharaohs would reenter the cloned body of themselves and live again.

The heart remained in the body to be removed only in the Hall of Judgment. When one dies, according to their Ausarian religion, after death, the heart is removed from the body and weighed in the "Hall of Judgment" to determine the Judgment of the soul for the God Ausar to allow passage into the afterlife *(heaven).* The Feather represents Truth.

The heart is placed on the left side of the scale and the feather is placed on the right side. Anubis checks the scale and if the heart is heavy, weighing more than the feather, then it would be devoured.

TEMPLE OF HATSHEPSUT

I knew nothing of Pharaoh Hatshepsut until my eyes became transfixed upon her Temple. The setting was flawless. She had it carved out of the foot of a glittering limestone mountain. One-thousand four hundred and seventy-eight years Before the Common Era (BCE). Then my eyes followed down to the floor of this unusual panorama to see an elegant three-level temple, carved directly into the footing of this extraordinary precipice. There was a long smooth ramp ascending from the floor of the courtyard going directly into the second-level terrace. The lower and upper levels were lined with columns from one end of the temple to the other. It looked like Washington, D.C.'s, Lincoln Memorial was modeled directly from one story of this elegant temple.

There were enormous statues of Hatshepsut along the walls of the temple. I noticed carvings on the walls depicting the god Amen impregnating Hatshepsut's Mother, Queen Ahmose to illustrate that she is truly the child of Amen-Ra. Therefore, unquestionably prepared to rulc as Pharaoh over Egypt. I learned that Hatshepsut had her architect erect the tallest obelisks in the world at the entrance to her temple. Egyptian Obelisks are normally placed in pairs at the entrance of adjourning temples. They are supposed to honor the god within the king or queen,

and to reflect on the vitality and immortality of the pharaoh. they are physical mirrors of the pyramids which are reminders of the god within each individual.

To this day, there is no evidence that our modern scientists have agreed upon how these obelisk stones, sometimes over a thousand pounds, were carved, how they were removed from their horizontal positions in the ground, how such a massive piece of stone was lifted and moved to their final designations, and then how they were finally positioned at their designation. This is thousands of years before the availability of any modern technology.

Hatshepsut inaugurated many structures throughout upper Egypt, but the gargantuan size of her own obelisk she had built inside the Temple of Karnak attests to the genius of her Architectural achievements. Her Temple was so revered that Pharaohs throughout Egypt chose to have their burial chambers constructed as near as they could to her site in the valley on the west side of the Nile River. This area became so popular that it was eventually named: "The Valley of Kings and Queens." Her memorial temple provides the entrance into the Valley.

Hatshepsut was the 3ʳᵈ female Pharaoh of Egyptian records with an impeccable bloodline. The ancient Egyptians were a matrilineal society wherein the lineage of their bloodline came down through the female side.

I learned late that the Persians Arab and Greeks who invaded Northeast Africa, mainly lower Egypt at that epoch, reversed the matrilineal line to the patrilineal. This meant that everything comes down through the male side and the woman has no basic rights except that which the male is willing to grant her. The royal succession and inheritance were then traced through the father rather than through the mother. This also was a significant point to me because the biblical Abraham, father of Judaism, Christianity, and Islam, was a paternalistic a Babylonian.

Hatshepsut's historical existence, becoming Pharaoh at age of 12, was practically erased from Egypt's archeological records by her adopted son. It is noted that she had a daughter with her husband, Thutmose II, but before he died, he fathered a non-Egyptian, illegitimate son— whom Hatshepsut adopted, making him a member of her royal family.

Thutmose III eventually married Hatshepsut's daughter of pure lineage.

After Hatshepsut's unexplained death, this adopted son became the Pharaoh and initiated the project of erasing her works including her name from all temples throughout Egypt. Her works including were so well buried that thousands of years later they, like her obelisk in Luxor, was uncovered in pristine shape.

I have to note here that what her adopted son, Thutmose III, did is what the Asians and Europeans were to do on a scale so grand that the history of ancient Egypt, as essentially black history, was essentially obliterated. He undertook to erase her name from all the monuments and temples she had built, destroying all documents bearing her name, and smashing all sculptured likenesses, paintings and, indeed anything that might indicate that Hatshepsut ever lived. Also, as later Europeans and Asians were to do to all inscriptions reflecting the Blacks, Thutmose III had his own name and that of his brother engraved where Hatshepsut's had been chiseled out, thus taking credit for all of her achievements in addition to his own outstanding works.

Hatshepsut's adoption of this illegitimate also put her on record for being the Pharaoh that ended the true, pure Egyptian genetic bloodline. The name Moses is not of Semitic origin but is intimately connected with the story of Isis, Osiris, and Horus. There were stories being passed through verbal history that Hatshepsut's illegitimate son's story parallels the story of the basket that Ah-Moses' Mother placed her baby in after she birthed Hatshepsut's husband's child. She put it into the Nile River as it was later recovered by Hatshepsut's daughter.

This story has its roots in the story of Isis and Osiris, the ancient religious ritual wherein Osiris was murdered and locked in a sarcophagus and dumped into the Nile River where he was rescued by his wife, Isis. Osiris is resurrected, and Isis immaculately births a son Heru/Horus. This became the original "First Holy Family" which Cultures and religions emulated.

It seems that there are countless references to the Egyptian cultic tradition for designating the future heir to the throne based on the story of Isis recovering Osiris from the river. The famous Babylonian story of King Sargon 2270-2315 BCE, found as a child floating in a basket in the river Euphrates, the Scandinavian King Skjold of Denmark; 26 Erechtonis of Athens; the Greek demigod Dionysus 27 who was found in Laconia; the Greek demigod 28 Attis; found by Cybele; the Indian Sun God's son; Karna; the Babylonian Queen Hammadi's son recovered from the Euphrates; the founder of Romulus, floating on the River Tiber; King Tu-kueh of Turkey; the legend of King Arthur; the children of the Celtic Kings on the River Rhine; as was the Japanese legends of Izanagis and Izanamis; newborn son.

King Sargon 2270-2325BCE

These ritualistic stories of being found floating in a basket, like the story of Moses, all originate from the first documented ritual tradition of Ancient Egypt.

THE TEMPLE OF KARNAK

"The Temple dedicated to the spiritual conception of Man"

Schaller De Lubicz p557

The Temple Of Karnak

The Master Builder Said To The Disciple:

"Know that everything that, of itself, diffuses outward without form needs a receptacle, Thus, Air retains the Fire of the Universe, and Water retains Air, as Earth is the vase that holds Water and gives it forms. Thus, Earth is the container of All."

The Temple of Karnak is dedicated to the spiritual conception of Man. His realization, the formation, is made in the womb.

THE TEMPLE OF MAN,
(Schwaller DeLubicz. P589)

THE Temple of Karnak was built to RETAIN the spirit of Man.

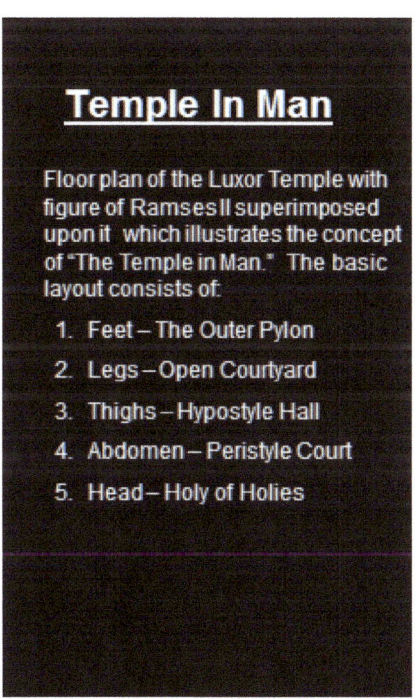

Temple In Man

Floor plan of the Luxor Temple with figure of Ramses II superimposed upon it which illustrates the concept of "The Temple in Man." The basic layout consists of:

1. Feet – The Outer Pylon
2. Legs – Open Courtyard
3. Thighs – Hypostyle Hall
4. Abdomen – Peristyle Court
5. Head – Holy of Holies

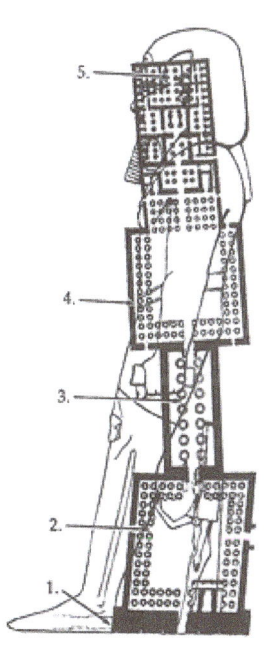

I was a bit puzzled as I noticed consistently how the woman was sculptured so small and placed at the foot of the gargantuan male statues. Then, after careful study, it dawned on me that the foot of the Temple. was the entrance to the temple. I factored in the quote from Schwaller DeLubicz: "Know that everything that, of itself, diffuses outward without form needs a receptacle." It only follows that "woman" is not only the receptacle but the very formation and realization of man. If I continue with Schwaller's realization, then woman is the container of All. LIFE EMANATES FROM THE WOMB.

Pharaohs are not only the ancestors of modern Egypt, but also the precursors of humanism...they built, studied imagined, discovered invented visualized, organized, lit the sacred fires of learning in an era when virtually the entire earth was still covered by a mantle of darkness. They overcame material constraints and grasped the spiritual dimensions thus enabling us to dream of eternity.

(Aly Maher El Sayed-Egyptian Ambassador)

I had toured the Great Sphinx, the Pyramids of Giza, the templesof: Esna, Edfu, Kom Ombo, Dendera, and Hatshepsut's temple. Each of these truly astounding sites were unbelievably prestigious, but then I entered the city of Luxor, the home of the Karnak Temple complex, the largest religious building in the world—over 200 acres in size along. There isn't a religious building in the world that compares to this amazing multiplex. The complex embodies thousands and thousands of years of African history. I was so overwhelmed that I had a hard time focusing that first day.

I could clearly see why the Karnak Temple was really a city of temples, a city of Gods, all enclosed in one monumental temple. Almost all the Pharaohs of the new kingdom left their signatures, statues, and cartouches for all posterity. The Presidents of our United States of America leave their signatures, statues, and pictures within the White House, but imagine if each of our Presidents built their own churches and instead of their pictures hanging on the wall of the White House, their individualized churches were inside 'The White House'.

This Great Temple was constructed in honor of the ram-headed creator God, 'AMEN'. The House wherein the God Amen resides. That's why the word Pharaoh originally meant House. I was stunned when the content director, Joshua J Mark, of the "World History Encyclopedia "published that "there was over 80,000 priests employed at Karnak by the end of the New Kingdom and the high priests there were wealthier than the pharaoh." Why isn't that information in any of "our" history books? *(Just asking)*

At the Temple's entrance, I faced an obelisk, 80 feet in height at the temple's entrance - there used to be two obelisks in front of all Egyptian Temples. The Arab Government of Egypt gave one to the United States, it is now standing in New York's Central Park. Not to be confused with the Washington Monument, a 555-foot marble obelisk, which was built to honor the United States first president.

 There were statues of African Pharaohs, but I felt dwarfed by the gargantuan obelisk pictured above, soaring over the whole compound. It belonged to Pharaoh Hatshepsut. Her adopted son had covered-up, built around much of her obelisk and erased other of her artifacts in order to wipe out any evidence of her existence - Sounds very familiar today. Ironically, the materials used to erase her only preserved her extraordinary history.

 It is quite understandable that the High Priesthood was more powerful and wealthier than any individual Pharaoh. This was true until the coming of the revolutionary Pharaoh, Amen**hotep** III. He eventually changed his name to Akhen**aten** to completely change the priesthood to focus upon the one God, Aten, the Sun god. His purpose was to use the Sun as a symbol of god since all life on the planet depends upon its light.

I was particularly stimulated by the 41-foot stature of Pharaoh Akhenaten. There were three categories of statues of him based on sizes from 41 feet to 28 feet. I was already curious about him when I Observed the complete stature of him in the Cairo Museum lobby.

Our tour guide explained to us how this African Pharaoh completely changed the destiny of the Egyptian Empire and set into motion the biblical foundation of modern monotheistic religions in the world today.

I must admit that this Pharaoh's African features, along with his wife Nefertiti and his son, Tutankhamen, aroused my sense of systemic betrayal. I felt betrayed by my formal educational system that granted me a college degree without revealing any knowledge regarding these historic figures in black skin, male and female gods who literally set the original stage for modern civilization.

Pharaoh Akhenaten lived at the peak of Egypt's glory. He came into the world, into Egypt to use that power to completely abandon if not to simply revolutionize traditionalism in Egypt. He eliminated the practice of Polytheism and returned the Egyptians to the original teachings that there is only one life, one God that's within each one. He used the powerful rays of the Sun, Aten, to demonstrate it as the source of life. This was the beginning of Monotheism as practiced today.

Akhenaten revolutionized ancient Egypts classical artistic expression into realistic Art. He adopted a pacifist attitude toward Egypt's powerful military, and in a sense, opened the gates of lower Egypt to the paternalistic Persians, Greeks, the Nomadic Hyksos, and the Romans. Then he rejected the gods of upper Egypt. He even removed their symbols, their statues, and names from all the temples except the Karnak Temple in upper Egypt, while compelling the temples to worship only one source of life, one God throughout the Egyptian Empire.

According to Gary Greenbery in "The Moses Mystery" The Egyptian Origins of the Jewish People, the Priesthood in upper Egypt rebelled against these abrupt changes causing the historic civil war between the two kingdoms of upper and lower Egypt. This war was won by the powerful Priesthood in Upper Egypt. They eventually Killed Akhenaten, destroyed his temple in lower Egypt, erased his emblems, statues, symbols and even his name. The High Priesthood of the city of Luxor and the Temple of Karnak had Akhenaten's young son, Tutankhaten, who became Pharaoh with the death of his father, return the capital's wealth and power to the High Priesthood in upper Egypt, to the temple of **Amen.**

The followers of Akhenaten agreed to leave lower Egypt after Akhenaten's death. Their mass exodus from lower Egypt documents the renowned biblical **Exodus**. This set the stage for western civilization by establishing the myth of Moses and the crucible for Judaism, Islam, and Christianity.

The Egyptian historian Manetho (3rd century B.C.E.), followed by Flavious Josephus (37-100 C.E.), the Roman historian Tacitius (36-107 C.E.), Sigmund Freud, and Joseph Campbell, asserted that the Moses of the Bible was not a Hebrew raised in the Egyptian palace but was an Egyptian Priest who led a religious revolution to establish monotheism.

In the Encyclopedia Britannica, scholars of Jewish history wrote:

"Although no external evidence proves that such a man named Moses lived, the subsequent history of Israel cannot be conceived without Moses, and his existence must be taken as a fact." (1996, p. 72)

The theory advanced by these historians was that after Akhenaten's death, his son, Tutankhaten, changed his name to Tutankhamen, then he helped reestablish the god Amen of upper Egypt. The 600,000 followers of Akhenaten agreed to leave Egypt rather than undergo punishment or death like their Pharaoh Akhenaten. His second in command Tuth-Moses, led them out of Egypt. This Exodus was rewritten as the biblical Exodus and the theology of Akhenaton was perpetuated and molded into present-day Judaism and Monotheism.

A Senegalese historian, anthropologist, physicist, and politician named Dr. Cheikh Anta Diop stated in the book "KEMET AND THE AFRICAN WORLDVIEW:"

After acquiring from African people all the elements of their future religion, tradition, and culture, including monotheism when they were ethnically, culturally, and Religiously an African people.

The most significant point of sharing the words of these reputable historians, is to unveil the myth that the Jewish people were enslaved by the ancient Egyptians, freed by the mythological Moses, the mass exodus of the Jewish people before there were Jewish people, the plagues, the crossing of the Red Sea, the 40 years in the desert, the Jewish conquest of the Promised Land, Moses as authoring the first five books of the bible—none of these storybook occurrences ever happened.

The biblical myth of Moses not only overshadows the great history of the people in black skins. A history that laid the foundation for western civilization, but it significantly laid the foundation for and the perpetuation of thousands of years of systemic racism.

I remember listening to what I considered to be a profound statement by a historian and pioneer in the creation of Pan-African Studies, Dr. John Henrik Clarke:

If you are the child of God and God is part of you, then in your imagination God is supposed to look like you. And when you accept the picture of the deity assigned to you by another people, you become the spiritual prisoners of that other people.

THE VALLEY OF THE KINGS

The VALLEY OF THE KINGS was like walking down into one of our modern-day malls. But the ancient Egyptian tombs were built without the modern technology. Modern-day Egyptologists have not been able to document how those ancient sites were built 3000 years Before Christ. At least 20 Pharaohs have been discovered entombed in this valley. Records indicate that our ancient Pharaohs used their most creative architects to craft these underground mausoleums for over 500 years. One of Ramsey's underground chambers had sixteen rooms in it!

I was simply amazed when I walked on the mountain path and stepped down into what looked like a cave, but it was Ramsey's underground mausoleum. Once I passed the dug-out entrance and went down the steps into the corridor, I observed scenes beautifully carved sacred texts illustrated impeccably on the walls and ceilings. I couldn't help noticing that the bodies in the scenes were all colored with red ochre.

I became focused on the word "colored" itself, noting that it embodied the words "color" and "red." The subject of the lighter-skin Colored Egyptians has garnered so much attention throughout the years that I couldn't help but think of my growing-up with Tarzan and movies with Elizabeth Taylor as Cleopatra with Richard Burton, etc., in the 1960s. I never imagined that there existed thousands of years of African Kings and Queens living in Black skins that led the world out of the jungles and into civilization.

I continued my descent into a second corridor with scenes depicting the Sun god's journey through the 12 divisions of the underworld, which are the 12 hours of the night,when the sun descends into the underworld in the western horizon and reappears as the newborn Sun in the East.

This mausoleum, I later learned,was one of the largest, around 8,800 square feet. While admiring theunending wall sculpturing, I stepped down into the burial chamber. I was surprisingly alone at the time, trying to take in all the detail I could handle. I focused on the wall sculpturing of the god Ausar (Osiris) and Anubis, the Jackal headed god that leads souls into the afterlife. While taking in the artistic splendor, I turned and looked up at Ramsey's sarcophagus that towered from the floor up and over my head, maybe a ten-foot-high sarcophagus. I felt a solemn moment overtaking me as

my knees weakened and I slowly bowed my head as I kneeled down on the floor. I could feel a thickness or denseness in the atmosphere and a lightness or better, an awareness on my body until I realized my whole body was levitating, it was slowly but definitely moving up alone the sides of the sarcophagus.

I suddenly knew I was slowly ascending into his sarcophagus. I wasn't unfamiliar with out-of-body experiences, and the blissfulness attached, but there was always an underlying apprehension of the return trip, getting back into the body. So, I caught myself, bonded with my physicality, grounded myself, feeling a little light-headed and hurried out of that burial chamber into the light of day. I returned to the cruise ship, entered my cabin and went into a blissful state of meditation until the ship departed.

PHILAE TEMPLE – Home of the "Immaculate Conception"

I contemplated the continual and extraordinary growth I was experiencing from cruising the Nile, visiting with the Great Sphinx, entering the Giza Pyramid, and visiting the temples at Esna, Edfu, and Kom Ombo. Ihad also disembarked in Aswan to see the "Unfinished Obelisk." That opportunity allowed me to see a giant obelisk in its formative stage which unleashed many questions like, how did they lift these solid stone granite obelisks weighing, over two million pounds? How did they carry it from Aswan to Hatshepsut's Temple and to Luxor, over a hundred sometimes miles away? Once they arrived, how did they stand it up? Even more important, how did they even sculpture it so perfectly?

This "Unfinished Obelisk" was 138 feet long. I tapped on it and heard its vibrations resonate like a gigantic tuning fork. The obelisk was unfinished because of an undesired crack in it, so it was never removed from its bedrock. Our tour guide indicated that it was ordered by the renown African female Pharaoh, Hatshepsut, around 1500 B.C.

But now our ship was docking to visit the temple of Isis on the Island of Philae. I got off the ship and walked over to about fifty very colorful docked small boats. They were white with blue railings; some also had red bottoms. The Nubian navigators were all dressed in white robes. Their skins were solid black, rich in melanin. They were very friendly and quite animated in filling their ferry boats with tourists. I jumped into the nearest boat and then looked at the Island perched in the center of the Nile River, with a temple, that looked like a castle, eclipsing the whole Island.

We all gathered around our tour guide once the total group arrived on the island. The guide began disclosing to us the story of Isis and her significance to the entire culture of Egypt, Greece, and Rome. However, he pointed out something incredibly special about this temple. It was the last refuge, where the ancient Egyptian culture survived after the Persian conquest, the Greek conquest, followed by the Romans. The last Egyptian Pharaoh to carve hieroglyphs on the temple walls was Nectanebo II, who died after Persia conquered Egypt, 343 B.C. The Greeks overtook the Persians in 332 B.C. and maintained control of Egypt under the Roman Empire into modernity.

I want to digress into a paragraph of history I've learned that helped me further appreciate my visit to this temple. When the Greeks seized Egypt, their generals were so astonished by its ancient culture, its monuments, art, and architecture that they found it wise to adapt to this amazing culture, centuries ahead of their own. General Alexander claimed himself to be pharaoh and his family, the Ptolemies, decided to build a new Egyptian capital in lower Egypt, Alexandria. They knew that to rule Egypt and its people, they had to be accepted and made part of the Ancient Egyptian sacred society, so Ptolemy I, Soter, not only adopted the title of pharaoh and had himself portrayed on the Egyptian monuments   in Egyptian style and dress, but they themselves completely duplicated traditional Egyptian dress and actions in every way except the language. (It is an interesting to note that Ptolemy's last name, Soter means Savior.) Although the Greeks completely dominated military, political, a n d economic control, they rarely integrated into Egyptian society and culture, they didn't speak the language. However, in lower Egypt, they adopted Egyptian customs, such as marrying their siblings.

According to Walter Williams in The Historical Origin of Christianity, they found a council of Ancient Egyptian priests and priestesses in lower Egypt who agreed to make an image of Ptolemy into a god by combining two Egyptian gods, Osiris and Apis the Egyptian sacred Bull, to create Oserapis—later Serapis, as the new god's name for Ptolemy I. This was the beginning of the creation of the religion of Christianity. They then built a Temple to honor their "Official God" named Serapeum after combining Serapis and Apis. The Greeks eventually achieved, with the help of the Egyptian Priesthood in lower Egypt, the skill of sculpturing themselves onto the Egyptian temple walls exactly as the indigenous Egyptians in black skins had done this since the 1st dynasty. However, I was somewhat perplexed with this two-dimensional image of the head of the Greek conquerors, Ptolemy I, depicting himself on the temple walls of Isis's Temple, wearing the White Crown of Upper Egypt, holding out his arms with an offering to the indigenous African god Horus. But I was informed, these Greek reliefs served the purpose of "validating" his descendance from the Egyptian gods. I continued to see such reliefs on temple walls throughout Egypt down through 300 years of colonialization. I still had to get used to seeing Greeks in clear white skins dressed in ancient indigenous Egyptian clothes, giving homage to Egyptian gods in black skins. I remember just standing before these scenes somewhat baffled.

The Greeks occupation of lower Egypt for 300 years was the source of the Pharaohs in white skin in Egypt from 305 B.C.E. – 30 B.C.E. This Greek Deity rule ended with the suicide of the Greek Queen Cleopatra in 30 B.C., 300 years later.

It was quite sobering for me to pick up a book by Chancellor Williams in 1987 called The Destruction of Black Civilization. He cited the vital reality of how that 300-year occupation of lower Egypt had the effect of completely eclipsing the historical achievement of people in black skins.

He described on page 98 how "The Asians and Europeans were so consecrated in lower Egypt, holding the seacoasts and thus blocking African contact with the rest of the world allowed them to perpetuate the myth that the remarkable achievements by people in black skin all over the continent, are attributed to the 'white Egyptians.' It was simply easy for them to appropriate exclusively not only the name Egyptian, but also all of the historical achievements made by the Egyptians in Black Skin throughout Egypt Ethiopian empire."

The tour guide now disclosed to us the mythical story and drama of this ancient royal family. The story of Isis, Osiris, and Horus which so saturated Egypt.

First, records from the pyramid texts, etc., documents that Osiris was the primeval king of Egypt. He set Egypt on the course of being the first if not one of the first civilizations of record. His name and statues have been located and verified in existence deep into central and southern Africa before the 1st Egyptian dynasty. As the king of Egypt, after bringing Egypt into a powerful unified Empire, he travelled to other regions to raise them to the standards of civilization as was done in ancient Egypt.

When he returned to Egypt, his brother Seth held a large festivity to honor his brother's return. Seth had set up a golden sarcophagus staged as a fantastic prize to anyone whose body could fit perfectly in the sarcophagus.

No match was found until he persuaded his brother to try it. Once Osiris got inside, he had his conspirators closed the lid, lock it, and then they threw it into the Nile River to sink away forever. However, Isis searched the waters and found the stone coffin and hid it in the woods. Seth heard she found the sarcophagus and this time he cut Osiris' body into 14 pieces and scattered them up and down the Nile throughout the kingdom. Isis searched again in a boat made of papyrus reeds. She found all the parts except the phallus which was eaten up by a fish.

Isis brought the pieces to this Temple on the island of Philae, and using her powers she prayed over the body, went into a trance and laid directly on its remains until she and Osiris was one God in one. Isis demonstrated how the powers she possessed within, combined with spiritual powers within Osiris allowed her to birth a new creation, a child that represented both she and Osiris. The child's name was Heru which is the source of our modern word Hero. The Greeks pronounced the name as Horus, born from a virgin, the immaculate conception.

While I was focused upon some pictographs/reliefs on the walls of the Temple, scenes were carved so perfectly on the stone walls that it was like reading a picture book when an older man, a Nubian, sitting along at the foot of the Temple, motioned with his fingers, for me to come to him. I walked over to him, and he asked if I would like to go into the Mamisi. That's the upper room where the divine birth took place. No one was allowed in that room. It wasn't even mentioned as a place we could enter on our guide. So, I was a little dumbfounded, why me, is it because I was the only person in black skin in that group? I nodded my head in the affirmative and he guided me up some stairs and pointed to the room but telling me I had only 10 minutes to get back.

I walked inside this sacred room and it felt like I was in another time. It was perfectly quiet. The carvings on the wall were so deep and so clear. They looked like they had just been carved. I felt I was truly on holy ground; I saw the body of Ausar/Osiris lying on a table that looked like the back of a lion. His sister Hathor was knelling at his head and another person wearing the headpiece of Auset/Isis was at his feet. Overhead was a bird a sparrow hawk flapping its wings as it seemed to be receiving the seed of Ausar/Osiris.

In another scene was a relief of Auset/Isis carrying a newborn Heru/ Horus in her arms. There were many more scenes on the four walls but I felt rushed, like I'd been in there hours, and I felt so comfortable, so subdued by the Aura that it was also a little frightening, that's hard to explain.

In conclusion, not only did I discover the significance of the "who" that's living in this black skin, but to gleam from this story, the power of this woman Auset/Isis. She not only had the persistence and determination needed to rescue her brother, husband, king, and God Osiris, but to be able to use her powers within to become one God /man/woman, who "Immaculately conceived the Hero-God Horus, the one who defeated the negativity of Seth without vengeance or hate. Because of this she is remembered and honored and became the god Isis for the Greeks, the Romans as well as her place as the Mother Goddess of the Ancient Egyptians. I can also say that she is the prototype for the Christian Virgin Mary.

As for the meaning of the story itself. Osiris had been king of the gods, but his brother Set, seeking the throne, arranged to have his brother eliminated. He did so by tricking him into getting into a sarcophagus, sealing it closed and floating it out to sea. In this manner, Set usurped the throne. Isis found the floating sarcophagus with the body, but her brother Set recovered it and cut it into pieces. However, Isis recovered all the pieces except the phallus, but she used her inner words of power to awaken Osiris' body. She then synced her powers with his and produced the son Horus. Fearing for the safety of the infant Horus, she hid away on a floating island. Horus, as the lawful heir to the throne, was raised with the prospect of avenging his father's death. Subsequently he challenged Set for the kingship, and after a series of battles defeated him.

The similarity between the Horus-Set theme and the biblical story of Moses comes into play. Ichnographically, Osiris is the displaced king, Set is the usurping king, Isis is the mother who hides the child away, and Horus is the returning son who defeats the usurping king. In the conflicting Egyptian and biblical versions, the pharaoh and Moses corresponds to either Horus or Set, depending upon which side tells the story.

The purpose of this mythological story is to keep in our consciousness Osiris' model as our True Self 's purpose in establishing order, harmony, and prosperity. Even when we're physically attacked, our spirit is still present even though we tend to focus upon our emotions and physicality. When our lower frequencies, which we symbolize as Set or Satan, tend to dominate our life, cutting the body into pieces is a simple metaphor for indicating a loss of a sense of unity, we mustn't forget our choice of using our will to stay balanced. When Osiris is thrown into the river it symbolizes the process needed to reintegrate our consciousness by simply being still and using our powers of visualization and meditation. Those words of power used by Isis to awaken our spirit gives us the choice of re-establishing ourselves. The body being thrown into the Nile River gives us the perfect visualization underwater of beginning the process of reintegrating our consciousness using meditation, trance, and visualization.

It must be noted here that the loss of Ausar's phallus/penis was remembered by incorporating the act of circumcision. Cutting the skin from the head of the phallus was symbolic of the cutting off Ausar's phallus. It is amazing that parents in modern times still cut off the skin around their male child's phallus without any clear explanation of where that religious practice originated.in remembrance of the story of Ausar.

THE ABU SIMBEL TEMPLE OF RAMSEY II

The most visited sight in Egypt after the pyramids, was the Great Temple of Ramsey II that was carved right out of the mountainside in Nubia, todays Sudan. This is an enormous rock temple complex located in a village in Nubia on the border of Sudan. I spent four days cruising down the legendary Nile River to visit this temple. I can honestly state that after the Pyramids, this complex was truly incredible. Upon disembarking I could only utter—WOW!

I stood with wide eyes trying to take in two whole temples carved right into a solid stone mountain, one dedicated to Ramsey II and the other dedicated to his wife, Nefertari. I was looking up at four seated carvings, each 33 feet high. Two on each side of the entrance.

I walked inside the 185-foot hallway observing four sculptured statues standing 32 feet high on each side of the hall. The hall leads into the Holy-of-Holy's chamber where four seated gods/statues, one being Ramsey II. The temple was so accurately constructed that twice a year, on Ramsey's II birthday, February 22, and again October 22, the day of his coronation, the rays of the sun penetrates the sanctuary and travels through the 185-foot hallway to the inner sanctum to illuminate the sculptures of Ra, Amun, and Ramses II. The 4th sculpture remains in the dark year-round because the god Ptah is the god of the underworld.

People from all over the world comes yearly to witness him being lit-up by the rising sun on his birthday.

A   B   C   D

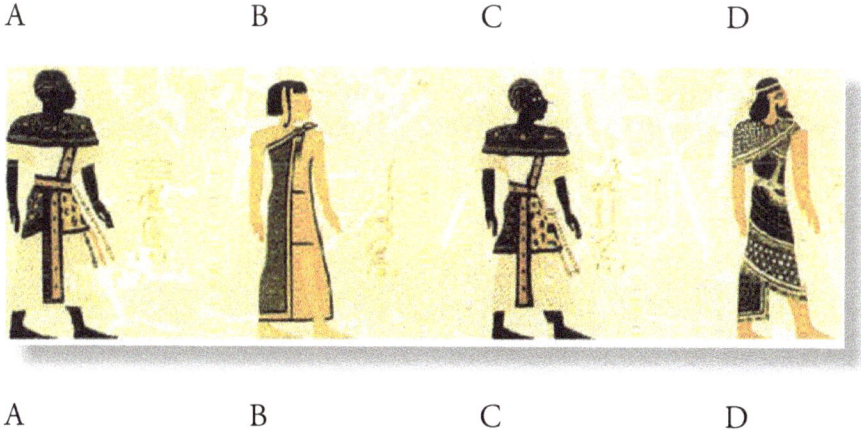

A   B   C   D

This painting from the tomb of Ramses III (1200 B.C.) shows that the Kemitians saw themselves as Blacks and painted themselves as such without possible confusion with the Indo-Europeans or the Semites. It is a representation of the races in their most minute differences, which ensures the accuracy of the colors. Throughout their entire history, the Egyptians never entertained the fantasy of portraying themselves by types B or D.

1.   The Egyptian seen by himself, black type C) The other Blacks in Africa

2.   The "Indo-European" D) The Semite

(From K.R. Lepsius: Denkmaler auk Aegypten und Aethiopien, Erganzungsband) plate 48

These words of Thoth, the Egyptian god of wisdom, found in the Hermetic texts, describing how the Gods chose the land of Kemit/Egypt as an image of heaven and its impending downfall.

"Did you know, (Imhotep), that Egypt is the image of Heaven. Moreover, it is the dwelling place of heaven and all the forces that are in heaven. If it is proper for us to speak the truth, our land is the temple of the world." This land, which once was holy, a land which loved the gods and wherein alone, in reward for her devotion, the god deigned to sojourn upon Earth: a land which was the teacher of mankind in holiness and piety…O Egypt, Egypt, of thy religion nothing will remain but an empty tale which thine own children in times to come will not believe, nothing will be left but graven words and only the stones will tell of the piety."

*Nag Hammadi Library

The Nag Hammadi library is a collection of early Christian and Gnostic texts discovered near the Upper Egyptian town of Nag Hammadi in 1945. Thirteen leather-bound papyrus codices buried in a sealed jar were found by a local farmer named Muhammed al-Samman.

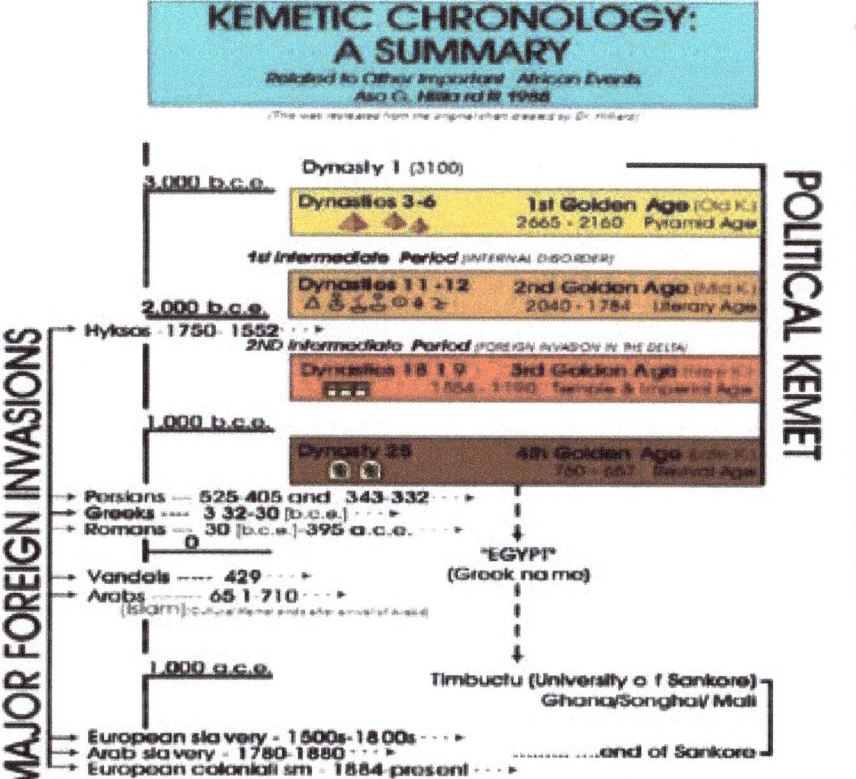

BIBLIOGRAPHY

Bauval R & A Brophy, Black Genius, The Prehistoric Origins of Ancient Egypt

Budge, Wallis, E. A., THE BOOK OF THE DEAD

Carruthers, Jacob A, KEMET, The African Worldview, Association for the Study of Classical African Civilizations, Edited by-Maulana Karenga – 1986

Casey, Edgar, Atlantis

Diop, Civilization or Barbarism,

Ellis, Ralph, Eden In Africa

Ellis, Ralph, Jesus Last of The Pharaohs

Ellis, Ralph, Tempest & Exodus

Ellis, Ralph, Thoth Architect Of The Universe

Fairbanks, Daniel I, Everyone Is African

Gordon, J., Egypt – Child of Atlantis

Greenberg, Gary, The Moses Mystery, The Egyptian Origins of the Jewish People

Haich, Elizabeth, Initiation

Holmes, Ernest, The Science of Mind,

Malkowsky, Edward F. Ancient Egypt 39,000 BCE

Melchizedek, Drunvalo, The Ancient Secrets of The Flower of Life

Moore, Webster, UCLA and the Angela Davis Case

Ramtha, A Master's Reflection on The History of Humanity

Roberts, Jane, Seth Speaks, The Eternal Validity of The Soul

Rinpoche, Guru, The Tibetan Book Of The Dead

Schwaller de Lubicz, R.A., The Temple of Man

Sertima, Van, Egypt Revisited,

Sitchin, The 12th Planet, Zecharia,1976, Avon books

The History of The Gods, Secharia Sitchin

Temple, Robert K.G., The Sirius Mystery, 1976,1987

Troward, Thomas, The Power In You

Thoth, Wells, The Keys of Enoch – The Book of Knowledge,

The Keys of Enoch – The Book of Knowledge,

Van Sertima, EGYPT Revisted

Williams, Walter, The Historical Origin of Christianity, 1992, Maathian Press Inc

Williams, The Destruction of Black Civilization

Discovering My Royal Heritage While Surviving in Black Skin

Reaching early adolescence in Mobile. Alabama, where responsible black people might be harassed or even killed if they dared to register to vote. Moore's parents hastily transplanted the entire family to California after the savage murder of young Emmett Till. evoking Moore's racial and cultural questioning. Even in California. he encountered racism as ingrained, hateful, and dangerous as it was in the South. His technically qualified father had to take work that prevented him from entering the homes of white people, and his mother would work as a maid for racially biased white folk. In high school. Moore was berated by a nun for suggesting gender equality and told that his brain size was "only a fifth of Caucasians." After military service. Moore became an influential teacher of Black studies and embarked on a deeply meaningful journey to Egypt and other African countries, where his view of himself and his race took on new meaning.

With photos, maps, language exploration, and a broad knowledge of the world and Christian history, Moore effectively shares his fresh perspectives. The ancient Egyptians who conceived and built the pyramids and created magnificent monuments such as the Great Sphinx were in fact, black people. Thousands of years of ancient black Egyptian history have been systematically replaced in favor of "400 years of slave history." The undeniable similarity between his facial features and those of the pharaohs further confirms a

Royal black heritage completely concealed from the history and origin of Western civilization. Moore's lively memoir can provide inspiration for persons of every skin color. It should easily prompt others to engage in their own research of the historical myth of race that's persistently used to justify the superiority of one human over another strictly based on the mere color of one's skin.

Barbara Bamberger Scott

US REVIEW OF BOOKS

www.ingramcontent.com/pod-product-compliance
Lightning Source LLC
Chambersburg PA
CBHW051630120626
46551CB00014B/2016